Patrick Novotny
The Parties in American Presidential Elections, 1789–2020

Patrick Novotny

The Parties in American Presidential Elections, 1789–2020

—

DE GRUYTER

ISBN 978-3-11-221550-0
e-ISBN (PDF) 978-3-11-134002-9
e-ISBN (EPUB) 978-3-11-134015-9

Library of Congress Control Number: 2023943726

Bibliographic information published by the Deutsche Nationalbibliothek
The Deutsche Nationalbibliothek lists this publication in the Deutsche Nationalbibliografie;
detailed bibliographic data are available on the internet at http://dnb.dnb.de.

Contents

To my wife, Theresa Beebe Novotny
To my parents, Margaret and John Novotny

Preface

The history of political parties in America's presidential elections is the history of America itself, and it is the history of a Constitution written by some of the most admired and respected figures of a generation of officeholders whose pleadings against political parties were rejected by ordinary Americans, taking it upon themselves to defy this discouragement and to form for themselves a party tradition whose history is as old as the Constitution itself. For all the talk of how much Americans respected President George Washington, they rejected his rejection of political parties in his famous Farewell Address of Monday, September 19, 1796 by sorting themselves in that very same moment into the 2 national parties then-shaping the country's 1796 election. The Federalists backing then-Vice President John Adams stood against the Democratic Republicans and their candidate, Thomas Jefferson. Looking back over 225 years, we know now what President Washington had no way of knowing at the time, that the parchment promises of our Constitution's words alone would not be enough, that they would be sustained not merely through the dedication and devotion of successive generations of Americans to the Constitution, but also through the large and loud institutions of America's political parties that through centuries of trial and tumult would allow ordinary citizens to form their own common purpose in the fiercely fought debates and in the heated campaigns and candidacies that came to define the nation.

We have the oldest written, continuously working Constitution in the world today because of our history of political parties in America, not in spite of them. Lawmakers in the first Congress assembled together in New York City's Federal Hall in the heart of what today is Wall Street in Lower Manhattan. They'd just heard President Washington's words delivered in the Senate chamber in his Thursday, April 30, 1789 Inaugural Address. In it, Washington rejected parties in no uncertain terms. "No separate views, no party animosities, will misdirect the comprehensive and equal eye which ought to watch over this great assemblage of communities and interests," Washington said in his Inaugural.[1] Members of the first Congress soon disregarded these words in their caucusing in the chambers of Federal Hall. Years later as he wrote his farewell remarks from his desk in the President's Mansion in Philadelphia in the Summer of 1796, Washington's parting words discouraging political parties were once again disregarded by his fellow Americans.

The Parties in American Presidential Elections, 1789–2020 is a book of some 30 years of teaching and writing about the place of political parties in America's his-

---

1 *The Gazette of the United States* Saturday, May 2, 1789, 3.

https://doi.org/10.1515/9783111340029-001

tory. I have always been fascinated with the idea of geography and of place in the study of our politics, and I could never have written *The Parties in American Presidential Elections, 1789–2020* without works like Kenneth C. Martis' *The al Atlas of the Political Parties in the United States Congress, 1789–1989.* The story told here in the pages of *The Parties in American Presidential Elections, 1789–2020* is a story that begins in New York City's Federal Hall and in the sessions of the first Congress. It is a story that includes the formation of the modern financial footings of the United States under then-Treasury Secretary Alexander Hamilton as well as the indispensable part of then-Rep. James Madison in his debates with Hamilton, debates that pitted New England against the mid-Atlantic and Southern states. America's financial foundations not to mention the very location of Washington, D.C. today were settled in Federal Hall by clashes that included geography and region in the Summer 1790 in the passage of Hamilton's Treasury bills and in the Residency Act passed for the location of the permanent capital on the banks of the Potomac River in parts of Maryland and Virginia.

The history of the remarkable revival of America's 2 party tradition in the mid- to late 1820s is told here in *The Parties in American Presidential Elections, 1789–2020* with careful attention to November 1824's election, an election that sprawls across the next 3 decades in the personalities and rivalries that dominated America's politics until the Civil War. 1828's defeat of President John Quincy Adams by Andrew Jackson, the founding of the Democratic Party and its long reach from the Southern states into Martin Van Buren's New York, and the rise of the anti-Jackson Whigs with names like Henry Clay, William Henry Harrison, Daniel Webster, and others are all stories told here in *The Parties in American Presidential Elections, 1789–2020*. So, too, is the history of 19th century Democratic, Whig, and Republican national party conventions, including the disastrous Democratic convention held in Charleston, South Carolina in April 1860 that adjourned as the only nominating convention of any major party in the country's history to ever adjourn without the selection of a Presidential ticket. Incumbent Presidents – 4 in all – were rejected by their national nominating conventions and refused re-nomination to run for a 2nd term. That this remarkable history of 19th century incumbent Presidents rejected by their party nominating conventions isn't highlighted in more accounts of this era's political parties is regrettable, but it is told here in some detail in *The Parties in American Presidential Elections, 1789–2020* as a part of the rich history of America's presidential elections.

In the years after the Civil War through the early years of the 20th century, America's Democrats and Republicans experienced a remarkable chapter of close-ly-fought elections contributing to election fraud and scandal unprecedented in our history. This fraud, in turn, drove a era of change and reform in America's elections, including voter registration laws and the beginning of standardized, state-printed ballots at the end of the 19th century. At the same time, primary elections began in a handful of states for selection of delegates to state conventions and eventually for the nomination of presidential tickets. Party-splitting primary challenges to the re-nomination of incumbent Presidents in these state-by-state primary contests – at least 3 or so of some consequence in the 20th century, including President William Howard Taft, President Lyndon Johnson, and President Gerald Ford – is a history highlighted here in the pages of *The Parties in American Presidential Elections, 1789–2020.*

Former President Theodore Roosevelt's party-splitting primary challenge to incumbent President William Howard Taft's re-nomination is the first of these 3 or so challenges to incumbent Presidents in the 20th century. Roosevelt's campaigning in the Spring of 1912 in a handful of states with Republican primary elections and then his unsuccessful bid for the White House that November as the presidential candidate of the Progressive Party helped to shape the beginning of a history of modern campaigning for Democrats and Republicans over the next century. Democrats in the 1920s and then Republicans in the 1930s both faced setbacks and stumbles that shook the confidence of party leaders, but both parties emerged resurgent in these moments. America's politics in the years after the 2nd World War saw party-splitting primary challenges to incumbent Presidents in the 20th century's continued growth of nominating caucuses and primaries, a new status quo in the long and winding path to the White House. America's politics in the years after the 2nd World War saw Democrats and Republicans also adapt ever more often to split-the-difference elections yielding divided government regularly in midterm elections from Presidents Harry Truman and Dwight Eisenhower through Presidents Barack Obama and Donald J. Trump.

Whatever else is said about America's Democrats and Republicans at the start of the 21st century, their history and that of earlier parties in the country's past tells a story of candidates and campaigning that is the story of the country itself. They tell us a story of clashes and compromises that take us all the way back to the hallways and the meeting rooms of the first Congress in New York's Federal Hall. Theirs is a story of the Civil War and of the fight for the survival of the union itself, and of the promise and the pursuit of citizenship for all. Theirs is the story of a people grasping the reins of their own government in times of peace and prosperity as well as in times of panic and peril. Theirs is a story of controversy and corruption. It is also a story of reform and reinvention. Their story is our story, their history is ours – for nothing in our Constitution and in our country's political past and its present is as close to the people themselves as their political parties.

Chapter 1 The Parties in the Early Republic, 1788 – 1800

The history of America's Constitution is the history of America's political parties. Stretching as far back as the colonial assemblies with their longstanding rival factions in the years before Independence, the history of today's political parties in America is most evidently and immediately rooted in the first Congress whose sessions in April 1789 saw the start of a long history of parties that traces to our own time. With members elected to the House of Representatives by a popular vote in their home districts and Senators selected by their state legislatures in the 11 states that had ratified the Constitution by this time, New York City's Federal Hall where the first Congress assembled is the most important starting place for the mix of personal rivalries, principled disagreements, and regional rifts that forged the first political parties under the Constitution.

Eleven states held the Constitution's first elections in the fall of 1788 and in the spring of 1789. Their competitiveness and the number of candidates running for each seat in the House in the first Congress varied from district-to-district and from state-to-state. Elections in these 11 states were mostly unremarkable affairs. Little actual campaigning took place in most states, and no real organization existed for most candidates in these first elections to the House. South Carolina and Pennsylvania's House elections in November 1788 were followed by mid- and late December races in New Hampshire, Massachusetts, and Connecticut – including the race for Massachusetts' first House District where the venerable Samuel Adams lost his bid for a seat in the first Congress to Fisher Ames.[2] January 1789's elections in Delaware and Maryland, February's elections in Virginia, Georgia, and New Jersey, and House contests in New York in March all elected members to the first Congress that spring.

Pennsylvania's rival tickets for the first Congress held the country's first party nominating conventions under the Constitution. Meeting in Harrisburg, delegates from 13 counties and the city of Philadelphia gathered on Wednesday, September 3, 1788 to nominate what became known as the Amendment list of House candidates for the first Congress.[3] Weeks later on Monday, November 3, 1788, a separate con-

---

2 *Massachusetts Centinel*, 20 December, in *The Documentary History of the First Federal Elections, 1788 – 1790, Volume I*, eds. Merrill Jensen and Robert A. Becker. The University of Wisconsin Press, 1976, 570.

3 "Resolved, that in order to prevent a dismemberment of the Union and to secure our liberties and those of our posterity, it is necessary that a revision of the Federal Constitution be obtained as soon as possible…That in order that the friends of amendments of the Federal Constitution, who

https://doi.org/10.1515/9783111340029-002

vention met in Lancaster, nominating a Federal ticket of candidates for House races as 16 different candidates in all vied for Pennsylvania's eight seats in the first Congress.[4] "These were the first nominating conventions ever held, the first application of the representative principle to party government," James S. Chase tells us in his definitive work, *Emergence of the Presidential Nominating Convention, 1789 – 1832*.[5] Virginia's ten House districts saw no fewer than 29 candidates for the first Congress make their case to voters, including in the second District on the far western edge of Virginia that today is the state of Kentucky. North Carolina's fifth House District stretched west into what is today the state of Tennessee. James Madison's campaign against James Monroe for Virginia's fifth House District – a campaign of horseback travel by Madison and Monroe in the frigid days of January and February 1789 to meetings in churches and courthouses including several appearances by the two candidates together to speak to crowds of voters – is a storied contest in these first races for seats in the first Congress.

New Jersey saw 14 candidates seek its four House seats in the first Congress, while in Georgia, the state's three districts saw a total of 16 candidates seek seats in the House for that state's Western or Upper district, its Central or Middle district, and its Lower District along the coast.[6] Delaware's single-seat in the House, one of just two states with only one seat in the first Congress, saw five candidates vie for

---

are inhabitants of this state, may act in concert it is necessary and it is hereby recommended to the several counties in the state to appoint committees who may correspond one with the other and with such similar committees as may be formed in other states," the first and third of four resolutions passed by the Harrisburg convention insisted. Proceedings of the Harrisburg Convention, 3 – 6 September, in *The Documentary History of the First Federal Elections, 1788 – 1790, Volume I,* eds. Merrill Jensen and Robert A. Becker. The University of Wisconsin Press, 1976, 260.

4 "Let the Constitution be fairly carried into execution, by those who are not its enemies, then such amendments, as experience may discover to be necessary, can be made without tearing the whole to pieces," James Wilson wrote in his report of the Lancaster convention. "The ticket, gentlemen, recommended on this occasion to your support, contains the names of George Clymer, Thomas Fitzsimons, Henry Wynkoop, Stephen Chambers, Thomas Heartly, John Allison, Thomas Scott, Frederick A. Muhlenberg." Proceedings of the Lancaster Conference, 3 November, James Wilson's Report of the Proceedings, in *The Documentary History of the First Federal Elections, 1788 – 1790, Volume I,* eds. Merrill Jensen and Robert A. Becker. The University of Wisconsin Press, 1976, 327.

5 James S. Chase, *Emergence of the Presidential Nominating Convention, 1789 – 1832*. The University of Illinois Press, 1973, 8. "So far as known, the conventions at Harrisburg and at Lancaster are the first State conventions in the United States held for the purpose of making nominations," Charles O. Paullin tells us. Charles O. Paullin, "The First Elections under the Constitution." *The Iowa Journal of History and Politics* 2, no. 1, January 1904, 7.

6 William Omer Foster, Sr., *James Jackson: Duelist and Militant Statesman, 1757 – 1806*. The University of Georgia Press, 1960, 69.

the seat.[7] Six more seats in the House would be filled a year later in contests in North Carolina in February 1790 and one seat later filled in Rhode Island in August 1790 as these states ratified the Constitution. In some districts, those running for seats in the new House saw little or no competition. Nearly all stood on their personal reputations and their service to their state assemblies or in other offices. Some had served in the Continental Congress or in the Congress of the Confederation.[8] Several members elected to the first Congress had served as delegates to 1787's Constitutional Convention. Their election to the first Congress offered them an extraordinary vantage to see firsthand the Constitution they'd worked so hard for in Philadelphia now set into motion in the chambers of Federal Hall.

"A quorum of the whole number of members being present, resolved, that this House will proceed to the choice of a Speaker by ballot," Thomas Lloyd's *The Congressional Register, or History of the Proceedings and Debates of the First House of Representatives of the United States of America* records for the first quorum for the House on Wednesday, April 1, 1789 with 30 of the elected 59 members present.[9] Elected with effectively no partisan affiliation, members of this first Congress arrived to the recently-renovated Federal Hall whose broad balcony and street-level entrance faced out to Wall Street. Members settled into the chambers of the House and the Senate with few premonitions of the rifts to soon divide the first Congress.

"It is not yet possible to ascertain precisely the complexion of the new Congress," Virginia Rep. James Madison wrote to his friend Thomas Jefferson on Sunday, March 29, 1789, only days before the first quorum in the House. "With regard to the Constitution, it is pretty well decided that the disaffected party in the Senate amounts to two or three members only, and that in the other House it does not exceed a very small minority," Madison told Jefferson.[10] "The members are principally solid moderate men," Rep. Fisher Ames observed weeks into the first Congress, though hinting too at a handful of House members as what Ames called "the Antis."[11] This handful of Representatives and Senators hinted at by Rep.

---

7 *The Documentary History of the First Federal Elections, 1788–1790, Volume I,* eds. Merrill Jensen and Robert A. Becker. The University of Wisconsin Press, 1976, 83.

8 James Roger Sharp, *American Politics in the Early Republic: The New Nation in Crisis.* Yale University Press, 1993, 31.

9 Thomas Lloyd, *The Congressional Register, or History of the Proceedings and Debates of the First House of Representatives of the United States of America, Volume I.* Harrison and Purdy, 1789, 3.

10 James Madison to Thomas Jefferson, Sunday, March 29, 1789, in *The Papers of James Madison, Volume XII, 2 March 1789–20 January 1790,* eds. Charles F. Hobson, William M. E. Rachal, Robert A. Rutland, and James K. Sisson. The University Press of Virginia, 1979, 38.

11 Fisher Ames to Samuel Henshaw, Wednesday, April 22, 1789, in *Documentary History of the First Federal Congress, 1789–1791. Correspondence, First Session: March-May 1789, Volume XV,* eds. Char-

Ames and others variously as the Anti-Federals or Antis, in a nod to the ratification debates still fresh in the minds of every member of the first Congress, had little organization in their ranks. As such, Madison, Ames, and others couldn't possibly have anticipated in these opening days of the first Congress just how much these divisions would grow in the months to come.

"The Galleries were open for the first time, and crowded," Ames wrote on Wednesday, April 8, 1789, just days into the first session of the House whose open doors welcomed not only curious locals from the sidewalks and streets of the surrounding neighborhood but also visiting delegations traveling from a distance, marking the first history of lobbying under the Constitution.[12] From all corners of the country as well as from curious New Yorkers wandering into Federal Hall, visitors made their way into the public gallery of the House. Almost immediately, the pages of the nation's papers filled with the latest reports of the debates in the House chamber, whose open doors and public gallery ensured that its deliberations would be reported in greater detail to the American people than almost any legislative body to that date. Four desks were placed in the back of the House chamber where reporters could listen to deliberations and write up their stories of the proceedings. "The laudable curiosity of the public is daily gratified by a free accession to the Galleries of the Hon. House of Representatives, where it is not doubted that the most profound attention and perfect decorum will continue to be exhibited by the spectators and auditors," *The Gazette of the United States* told its readers on Saturday, April 18, 1789.[13] Items and news stories soon filled the nation's papers on deliberations in the House, often reprinted from John Fenno's *The Gazette of the United States* sold on Wednesdays and Saturdays from his shop at No. 9 Maiden Lane.

Many of those members elected to serve in the first Congress to forge the new national government spoke and wrote at some length with a disdain for the idea of political parties. In some of these writings, the word party is often used interchangeably with words like faction or interest. Interest was often capitalized in such commonplace colloquialisms as the Federalist Interest or the Anti-Federal Interest, or sometimes un-capitalized, like the republican interest. Words like cabal, conclave, or even words like monster (the antifederal Monster), specter (the Spec-

lene Bangs Bickford, Kenneth R. Bowling, Helen E. Veit, and William Charles DiGiacomantonio. The Johns Hopkins University Press, 2004, 314.

12 Fisher Ames to James Lowell, Wednesday, April 8, 1789, in *Documentary History of the First Federal Congress, 1789–1791. Correspondence, First Session: March-May 1789, Volume XV*, eds. Charlene Bangs Bickford, Kenneth R. Bowling, Helen E. Veit, and William Charles DiGiacomantonio. The Johns Hopkins University Press, 2004, 221.

13 *Gazette of the United States* Saturday, April 18, 1789, 3.

ter of Antifederalism) or sect were used at this time to describe these still-emerging parties in their earliest iterations. Publicly, most lawmakers in the first Congress expressed a disdain and distrust of parties. Less publicly, some of these same House and Senate members quietly worked behind-the-scenes to form the soon-to-emerge caucuses in the first Congress.

"The proceedings of the new Congress are so far marked with great moderation and liberality," Rep. James Madison wrote from New York to his friend Thomas Jefferson on Wednesday, May 27, 1789, "and will disappoint the wishes and predictions of many who have opposed the Government."[14] That May, one visitor spending time in the gallery of the House, North Carolina's Tristram Lowther, observed the "great liberality of sentiment and spirit of mutual concession" of House members. "I have not observed," Lowther said, "the least attempt to create a party, or to divide the House by setting up the Southern in opposition to the Eastern interest, except in a Mr. Jackson from Georgia, the violence of whose passions sometimes hurries him into expressions which have, or appear to have, such a tendency."[15] A fierce opponent of some of the revenue measures debated that Summer of 1789 and outspoken too against Rep. Madison's proposed Amendments to the Constitution, Jackson's speeches from the floor of the House were said to rattle the windows of his own chamber downstairs in Federal Hall and stir no small measure of unhappiness with Senators hearing Jackson's words carry into their own chamber upstairs.

In the summer of 1789, members of the House and the Senate in the first Congress worked to put the new national government in motion. *The Gazette of the United States* filled with the latest news of bills passed by the first Congress creating new departments. The Departments of Foreign Affairs, Treasury, and War were each created that summer. News of the passage of bills establishing each department and of President Washington's nomination of his cabinet members filled columns in the papers each day out of New York. Passage of the Judiciary Act put in motion the selection and sitting of the first Chief Justice of the Supreme Court, John Jay, and the court's first Associate Justices to serve on the bench.[16] Debates over the permanent location of the capital sparked some early disagreements in

---

14 James Madison to Thomas Jefferson, Wednesday, May 27, 1789, in *The Papers of James Madison, Volume XII, 2 March 1789–20 January 1790*, eds. Charles F. Hobson, William M. E. Rachal, Robert A. Rutland, and James K. Sisson. The University Press of Virginia, 1979, 186.

15 Tristram Lowther to James Iredell, Saturday, May 9, 1789, in *Documentary History of the First Federal Congress, 1789–1791. Correspondence, First Session: March-May 1789, Volume XV*, eds. Charlene Bangs Bickford, Kenneth R. Bowling, Helen E. Veit, William Charles DiGiacomantonio. The Johns Hopkins University Press, 2004, 493.

16 *Gazette of the United States* Wednesday, September 30, 1789, 3.

these months, but the enactment of July 1789's tariff measure and that September's passage of Madison's Amendments to the Constitution were moments of the first Congress done before the party rifts soon to form.

"There is less party spirit, less of the acrimony of pride when disappointed of success, less personality, less intrigue, cabal, management, or cunning than I ever saw in a public assembly," Rep. Ames said of the House in July 1789. Ames observed "some sparks of faction" among members of the House, but "they went out for want of tinder."[17] "Much harmony, politeness, and good humor have hitherto prevailed in both houses," Rep. William Smith of South Carolina wrote at almost the same time. "Our debates are conducted with a moderation and ability extremely unusual in so large a body," Smith wrote. "How long this delightful accommodation will continue is uncertain," he said. "I sincerely wish I shall never see it interrupted."[18] Contrary to Rep. Smith and others, Speaker Frederick A. Muhlenberg hinted at the coalescing of alliances in the House. "The Antis now begin to discover themselves, and they are on this Occasion bringing their whole force to a point. I think I see an antifederal Monster growing, which if it should gain Strength will I fear interrupt the Harmony with which we have hitherto proceeded," Speaker Muhlenberg wrote on Thursday, June 18, 1789, a premonition of the divisions in the House chamber still some months away.[19]

That Fall, the first Congress grew more fractured as members braced themselves for the fiscal measures being assembled by Alexander Hamilton, who took the helm of the Treasury in September 1789 and was almost immediately thrown into the center of the growing division in the ranks of Congress as he prepared his much-anticipated report on the federal treasury. Whispers of alliances being formed by like-minded lawmakers in the House were heard for the first time. The Treasury Secretary's supporters in the House were known to some as

17 Fisher Ames to George R. Minot, Wednesday, July 8, 1789, in *Documentary History of the First Federal Congress, 1789 – 1791. Correspondence, First Session: June-August 1789, Volume XVI*, eds. Charlene Bangs Bickford, Kenneth R. Bowling, Helen E. Veit, and William Charles DiGiacomantonio. The Johns Hopkins University Press, 2004, 978.

18 William Smith to Gabriel Manigault, Sunday, June 7, 1789, in *Documentary History of the First Federal Congress, 1789 – 1791. Correspondence, First Session: June-August 1789, Volume XVI*, eds. Charlene Bangs Bickford, Kenneth R. Bowling, Helen E. Veit, and William Charles DiGiacomantonio. The Johns Hopkins University Press, 2004, 718.

19 Frederick A. Muhlenberg to Richard Peters, Thursday, June 18, 1789, in *Documentary History of the First Federal Congress, 1789 – 1791. Correspondence, First Session: June-August 1789, Volume XVI*, eds. Charlene Bangs Bickford, Kenneth R. Bowling, Helen E. Veit, and William Charles DiGiacomantonio. The Johns Hopkins University Press, 2004, 807.

the Hamilton gallery, still others proclaiming themselves the Secretary's Party.[20] The military language of commanders, generals, gladiators, sergeants, squadrons, and troops – all in reference to Secretary Hamilton and his supporters – spoke to a deepening rift in the first Congress late that Fall as loosely organized affiliations of members increasingly took form.[21] In hallway conversations and in meetings of all manner in the late fall of 1789 and the early spring of 1790, members of the House and their counterparts in the Senate braced themselves for a debate far greater than any to date in the first Congress.

President George Washington's first annual message to Congress – what we know today as the State of the Union – delivered by the President on the morning of Friday, January 8, 1790 was followed just days later by the delivery to the House of the much-anticipated report by Treasury Secretary Hamilton on the finances of the federal government.[22] *Report of the Secretary of the Treasury to the House of Representatives, Relative to a Provision for the Support of the Public Credit of the United States* sparked a debate unlike any other in the first Congress, and formed the foundations for the first true party caucuses. Secretary Hamilton submitted his report on the Treasury Department, accompanied by bills in the House and the Senate introduced by the Secretary's supporters to enact the proposed new fiscal and revenue measures. Hamilton hoped to build on the successes of 1789's tariff bill with additional imposts, along with laying an excise "upon Spirits distilled within the United States" for every gallon of domestically produced alcohol.[23]

---

20 Still other diaries, letters, and records kept by members of the first Congress – especially that of Senator William Maclay of Pennsylvania – describe Representatives and Senators supporting the Treasury Secretary as the Secretary's group or, in Senator Maclay's words, "the Partizans of the Secretary." "I never observed so drooping an Aspect, so turbid & forlorn an appearance, as overspread the Partizans of the Secretary in our House this forenoon," Senator Maclay wrote in his journal on Thursday, April 8, 1790. "If I had chose to Use the Language of political Scandal, I would call them the Senatorial Gladiators." Thursday, 8 April 1790, in *Documentary History of the First Federal Congress of the United States of America, 1789–1791. The Diary of William Maclay and Other Notes on Senate Debates, Volume IX, eds.* Kenneth R. Bowling and Helen E. Veit. The Johns Hopkins University Press, 1988, 239.

21 "[Thomas] Jefferson lamented that the Hamiltonians exhibited in Congress all the precision of a squadron," John C. Miller tells us in 1960's *The Federalist Era, 1789–1801.* John C. Miller, *The Federalist Era, 1789–1801.* Harper and Brothers Publishers, 1960, 123.

22 "The House being assembled, adjourned to the Senate Chamber. At 11 o'clock, THE PRESIDENT of the United States, attended by his Aides, and Secretary, was received by the two Houses of Congress in the Senate Chamber," *The Gazette of the United States* reported. *Gazette of the United States* Saturday, January 9, 1790, 3, Capitalization in original.

23 *Report Relative to a Provision for the Support of Public Credit, Saturday, January 9, 1790,* in *The Papers of Alexander Hamilton, Volume VI, December 1789-August 1790,* eds. Harold C. Syrett and Jacob C. Cooke. Columbia University Press, 1962, 102–103.

Looming larger still was the debate on the state treasury debts carried over from the War of Independence, debts that Secretary Hamilton argued should be assumed from the states by the national Treasury.

"Though our present debt be but a few millions, in the course of a single century, they may be multiplied to an extent we dare not think of," Rep. James Jackson said in floor debate in the House on Tuesday, February 9, 1790, pushing back against the Treasury Secretary.[24] Madison, Jackson, and other House members rallied the Treasury Secretary's opponents to reverse the initial passage of Hamilton's bill. Madison held together his opposition ranks to reverse the bill's initial passage by a 31 – 26 vote on Tuesday, March 9, 1790, with a vote now defeating it by 29 – 27 in the House on Monday, March 29, 1790.[25] "A Public Debt is a Public curse and in a Rep. Govt. a greater than in any other," Madison wrote on Tuesday, April 13, 1790, as the resolve of the opposition ranks stiffened days after the defeat for Hamilton.[26] Higher indebted states – led by Massachusetts and its Representatives in the House – appealed to their colleagues by reminding them that state debts like theirs had been accumulated during the War of Independence.

"In the name of the People of Massachusetts, who have honored me with the seat in this House, in whose behalf my colleagues and myself have united in representing their services and sufferings, do I address you," Rep. Theodore Sedgwick said to the House, as he took to task his fellow House members for not allowing the national Treasury to assume the debts of states like his that had suffered some of the highest costs of troops and material during the war. "We have demanded justice, we have implored the compassion of the Representatives of the People of America, to relieve us from the pressure of intolerable burdens, burdens incurred in support of your freedom and independence," Sedgwick told his fellow House members in appealing for passage of the Treasury Secretary's bill.[27] Whispers of backroom deals being sought by the Treasury Secretary and even talk of secession if the Secretary's bill passed spoke to the divisions and the suspicions swirling in the House that Spring.

---

24 Thomas Lloyd, *The Congressional Register, or History of the Proceedings and Debates of the First House of Representatives of the United States of America, Volume II.* Hodge, Allen, and Campbell, 1790, 255.

25 Orin Grant Libby, "A Sketch of the Early Political Parties in the United States." *The Quarterly Journal of the University of North Dakota* 2, no. 3, April 1912, 217.

26 James Madison to Henry Lee, Tuesday, April 13, 1790, in *The Papers of James Madison, Volume XIII, 20 January 1790 – 31 March 1791,* eds. Charles F. Hobson, William M. E. Rachal, Robert A. Rutland, and James K. Sisson. The University Press of Virginia, 1981, 148.

27 *Gazette of the United States,* Wednesday, April 14, 1790, 2.

Opponents of the Treasury Secretary in the House held their ground and grew the ranks of the opposition, much to the frustration of House members supporting Hamilton's assumption bill.[28] Speaker Frederick A. Muhlenberg stood with the anti-assumptionists, sending shudders through the ranks of Hamilton's House supporters.[29] "Mr. Madison has departed so exceedingly from his federal principles [that] the luster of his character declines," one figure wrote angrily in the pages of Saturday, April 17, 1790's *The Gazette of the United States*.[30] Tempers flared. Tensions mounted. Tragedy was averted following a heated exchange between Rep. Aedanus Burke of South Carolina and Treasury Secretary Hamilton as the threat of a duel between the two men dissipated with their exchange of apologies.[31]

By the early summer, Treasury Secretary Hamilton's assumption bill stood at an impasse. Negotiations between Hamilton and Madison that June finally broke this impasse, opening the door for the House to take up the consideration of the assumption bill once again. Taking their first tentative steps to a compromise, House members hammered out an agreement to temporarily locate the capital in Philadelphia while the location of a permanent place for the government was agreed to on the banks of the Potomac River from land in Maryland's Montgomery County and Prince George's County and from Virginia's Fairfax County.

Friday, July 16, 1790's enactment of an Act for Establishing the Temporary and Permanent Seat of the Government opened the door to the subsequent compromise on Secretary Hamilton's debt assumption measure. Wednesday, July 21, 1790's passage of the assumption bill in the Senate by a 14 – 12 vote brought the impasse still closer to some closure. Wednesday, August 4, 1790's assumption bill finally passed in the House, with a handful of members from Maryland, New Jersey, Pennsylvania, and Virginia switching their votes and now casting them in favor of

---

28 "Whatever regard the members may have had for each other's feelings had pretty much disappeared," Ralph Volney Harlow tells us of the rifts in the House by March 1790. "'Violence, personality, low wit, violation of order, and rambling from the point' characterized at least one debate. Apparently, the discussion took such a bitter turn that the papers did not venture to report in full." Ralph Volney Harlow, *The History of Legislative Methods in the Period before 1825*. Yale University Press, 1917, 138.

29 Roland M. Baumann, "'Heads I Win, Tails You Lose': The Public Creditors and the Assumption Issue in Pennsylvania, 1790 – 1802." *Pennsylvania History* 44, no. 3, July 1977, 206.

30 *Gazette of the United States* Saturday, April 17, 1790, 3. "The slow progress in public business excites very general concern," *The Gazette of the United States* told its readers. "The Anties laugh. The friends to the National Government mourn." *Gazette of the United States* Wednesday, April 14, 1790, 3.

31 Aedanus Burke to Alexander Hamilton, Wednesday, April 7, 1790, in *The Papers of Alexander Hamilton, Volume VI, December 1789-August 1790*, eds. Harold C. Syrett and Jacob C. Cooke. Columbia University Press, 1962, 358.

the measure.[32] By that November, with revenues starting to fill its coffers, Treasury Secretary Hamilton finally began repaying debt to the French government, the first such payment by the United States of its debt to domestic and foreign creditors that continues uninterruptedly to this day.[33] A Constitution forged out of compromises in 1787's Summer now forged its first historic compromises in the Summer of 1790 for the financial footings of the new government and for the permanent location of its national capital.

The capital's move from New York to Philadelphia came on the eve of 1790's Congressional midterms, at a time when the divisions sharpened between the caucuses in the first Congress.[34] Newspapers and their printers aligning with these rifts between the members of first Congress took on an even greater prominence. John Fenno moved his *Gazette of the United States* to Philadelphia at a shop at No. 69 Market Street. Essays and writings signed and unsigned in the pages of *The Gazette of the United States* frequently favored the Treasury Secretary and his supporters in Congress. Within weeks of Congress' move to Philadelphia, Benjamin Bache, grandson of the late Benjamin Franklin, issued the first printing of his *Aurora* from his print shop at No. 112 Market Street. Essayists in *The Aurora* spoke often on behalf of those opposed to Secretary Hamilton and against Vice President Adams, drawing the ire of its printer's powerful critics in years to come. Closed to the public for another five years still, the Senate's chamber upstairs on the second floor of Congress Hall yielded only the occasional item in Philadelphia's papers, but House proceedings from the first floor's chambers and the day-to-day deliberations of its members were widely-read in the pages of *The Gazette of the United States*, *The Aurora*, John Dunlap's *Dunlap's American Daily Advertiser*, and other newspapers.

1790's midterm contests for most incumbent members of the House marked the affiliation of some lawmakers for the first time with one or the other of the two caucuses now settling into the first and second floors of Congress Hall.

---

32 Orin Grant Libby, "A Sketch of the Early Political Parties in the United States." *The Quarterly Journal of the University of North Dakota* 2, no. 3, April 1912, 217–218.

33 Samuel Flagg Bemis, "Payment of the French Loans to the United States, 1777–1795." *Current History* 23, no. 6, March 1926, 828.

34 The first Congress' caucuses in the House saw a settling and a sifting and a sorting of some 37 Administration members pitted against some 28 Anti-Administration House members, according to Kenneth C. Martis' definitive *The Historical Atlas of the Political Parties in the United States Congress, 1789–1989.* In the Senate, 18 Administration members, by Martis' count, held the majority in that chamber – with a scattering of some eight Anti-Administration Senators, including two from Georgia, two from Vermont, and one each from Delaware, New Hampshire, Pennsylvania, and Rhode Island. Kenneth C. Martis, *The Historical Atlas of the Political Parties in the United States Congress, 1789–1989.* Macmillan Publishing Company, 1989, 70.

Eight sitting members of the House were defeated in 1790 – some from the ranks of supporters of the Treasury Secretary, some from the ranks of his opponents. Two Hamilton-supporting House incumbents lost their seats in Maryland, with opposition challengers winning in Maryland's third and sixth House districts. In New York, an opposition incumbent lost that state's sixth District to a supporter of the Treasury Secretary, while an opposition challenger defeated an incumbent supporter of Hamilton in New York's fourth District. South Carolina's second district saw a pro-Hamilton challenger defeat an opposition incumbent in the race for that House seat.[35] Unremarkable as 1790's midterm election appeared at the time, the first elections under the new government to have the defeat of incumbent office-holders was an extraordinary moment in the history of the Constitution, the first transfers of power at the district level as the first sitting House members lost their seats and gave up their places in the House to their opponents.

In December 1790, the lame-duck House turned its attention to Treasury Secretary Hamilton's proposal for the chartering of a Bank of the United States. The Secretary's proposal faced yet another backlash from the opposition in Congress.[36] Hamilton's loyalists did their best not to be outflanked by Madison and his caucus.[37] Opponents of the Treasury Secretary took to calling their House rivals the English Party, in part, for Hamilton's praise of the Bank of England, while others called them the Court Party.

A bitterly divided Congress in February 1791 finally passed the bill to establish a Bank of the United States. Attorney General Edmund Randolph and Secretary of State Thomas Jefferson urged the President to veto the bill. From the House, Madison also pleaded with Washington to veto it. As with the assumption bill, Washington's Treasury Secretary stood by his measure, and urged the President to sign his bill into law. Following Hamilton's advice and signing the Bank of the United States bill into law on Friday, February 25, 1791, President Washington saw the opening of the doors of the Bank of the United States on Philadelphia's Third

---

35 Stanley B. Parsons, William W. Beach and Dan Hermann, *United States Congressional Districts, 1788–1841.* Greenwood Press, 1978, 2–31. The second Congress whose session began in March 1791 saw 39 Administration members holding the majority to some 30 Anti-Administration opposition members in the House. In the Senate, 16 Administration Senators and Thirteen Anti-Administration Senators served in that chamber. Kenneth C. Martis, *The Historical Atlas of the Political Parties in the United States Congress, 1789–1989.* Macmillan Publishing Company, 1989, 71.
36 "There were plenty of opposition votes," Orin Grant Libby tells us, "but they were so scattered, both as to measures and as to delegations, that they can hardly be said to show much evidence of organization." Orin Grant Libby, "Political Factions in Washington's Administrations." *The Quarterly Journal of the University of North Dakota* 3, no. 4, July 1913, 300.
37 Ralph Volney Harlow, *The History of Legislative Methods in the Period before 1825.* Yale University Press, 1917, 155.

Street, a building which today stands mostly forgotten, mere blocks from Independence Hall. To this day, the old Bank of the United States building stands as an architecturally elegant but largely forgotten witness to a history of the once-fierce debates surrounding this chartering of a national bank in the young republic.[38]

Discouraged by their defeat on Friday, February 25, 1791 when President George Washington signed into law the Bank of the United States bill, Secretary of State Thomas Jefferson and Rep. James Madison left Philadelphia soon after and spent several weeks traveling through New York, Massachusetts, Connecticut, and New Jersey, thought by some of their rivals to be the first steps by the Virginians to form a full-fledged opposition political party to take on the supporters of Secretary Hamilton.[39]

"Their itinerary took them from New York up the valley of the Hudson River to Lake George and Lake Champlain, across Vermont and down the Connecticut River valley, returning by way of Long Island," historian Merrill D. Peterson tells us. "This was fresh country for the Virginians."[40] Hamilton and his supporters carefully watched the travels of Jefferson and Madison, a trip that at the end of the day yielded little if any immediate political inroads for the Virginians, but no doubt laid the groundwork for alliances to come with the supporters of the Virginians in the Northeast.

President George Washington's well-known frustrations with these deepening partisan currents led to his own hesitance to stand for reelection in 1792. Distrust seemed to grow in the hallways of Congress Hall in the months leading up to the presidential election. Anonymous essays in *The Gazette of the United States, The Aurora, Dunlap's American Daily Advertiser*, and other papers offered sometimes thinly disguised aliases for some of the most prominent lawmakers of the day, including those at the highest levels of the Executive branch such as Vice President Adams and Secretary Hamilton, whose unsigned writings embarrassed and frustrated President Washington to no end.

"The votes which have been given in the respective states for Vice President will decide the fate of the National pulse as to federal principles," Saturday, Janu-

---

38 *The Gazette of the United States* Wednesday, March 2, 1791, 3.
39 *Gazette of the United States* Wednesday, June 8, 1791, 3.
40 Merrill D. Peterson, *Thomas Jefferson and the New Nation: A Biography.* Oxford University Press, 1970, 439. "Hamilton and his friends imagined political intrigue where there was none," Peterson insists, explaining to his readers that George Clinton, in Peterson's words, "seems not to have noticed the touring Virginians, nor did they call on him." "If any alliances or bargains were struck," Peterson adds, "they were very secret indeed, for they left no trace." Merrill D. Peterson, *Thomas Jefferson and the New Nation: A Biography.* Oxford University Press, 1970, 440

ary 5, 1793's *The Gazette of the United States* told its readers, culminating months of maneuvering that brought a partisan rift into that year's reelection of President George Washington.[41] Standing for reelection unopposed as President Washington did in 1792, supporters of then-Rep. James Madison and others used their network to organize lawmakers in some states to use the second of the 2 Electoral votes cast by each state's Electors under Article II of the Constitution to mount an unusual electoral challenge to Vice President John Adams' reelection. Splitting the second set of votes cast by Electors as provided under the Constitution's Article II, Section 1 gave an unusual opening for the opposition to challenge Vice President Adams' reelection.

Months earlier, correspondence and meetings to coordinate this challenge to Vice President Adams – including a meeting in Philadelphia on Tuesday, October 16, 1792 of opponents of Vice President Adams from New York, Pennsylvania, South Carolina, and Virginia – had choreographed this casting of the second of the two Electoral votes cast by Electors in several states.[42] Massachusetts' John Hancock and New York's Aaron Burr both were among those who'd been considered as candidates for challenging the Vice President, but Madison and others backed the New York Governor. Clinton's backers expressed their certainty in President Washington's reelection, even as they lined up the casting of the second Electoral votes from five states. Georgia, New York, North Carolina, Pennsylvania, and Virginia all cast votes for Vice President for Gov. Clinton. In the end, Adams' 77 Electoral votes for the nation's second highest office to Clinton's 50 ensured Adams a second term as Vice President, and all but assured his race four years later for President.[43]

House races of 1792, with some 36 new seats in the House from 1790's Census apportionment as well as the expansion of the union to include Kentucky and Vermont, brought a larger, more boisterous House, one shaped even more by the partisan allegiances of its members.[44] For the first time under the Constitution, an op-

---

41 *Gazette of the United States* Saturday, January 5, 1793, 3.

42 "A Meeting was had last evening between Melancton Smith, on the part of the republican interest of NY (specially deputed) and the principal movers of the same interest here, to conclude *finally & definitively* as to the choice of a V.P., the result of which was, unanimously, to exert every endeavor for Mr. Clinton, and drop all thoughts of Mr. Burr," John Beckley wrote to Rep. James Madison the day after Tuesday, October 16, 1792's Philadelphia meeting. John Beckley to James Madison, Wednesday, October 17, 1792, in *The Papers of James Madison, Volume XIV, 6 April 1791–16 March 1793*, eds. Robert A. Rutland, Thomas A. Mason, Robert J. Brugger, Jeanne K. Sisson, and Fredrika J. Teute. The University Press of Virginia, 1983, 383, Italics in original.

43 *Gazette of the United States* Saturday, February 16, 1793, 2.

44 Kenneth C. Martis, *The Historical Atlas of the Political Parties in the United States Congress, 1789–1989.* Macmillan Publishing Company, 1989, 72.

position majority ("the party which distinguishes itself by an opposition to the government of the United States," as Wednesday, March 13, 1793's *The Gazette of the United States* declared it) won control of the House. The opposition won a slim 54–51 margin of House seats in the third Congress in the same election that returned President George Washington to his second term.[45] The election in 1792 is the first election under the Constitution where voters give the nation divided government – as the same election that President Washington won reelection saw a three-seat margin for the opposition House members to take control of that chamber.[46] Rep. Frederick A. Muhlenberg eventually took his post as Speaker elected by this new opposition in the House chamber.[47]

1794 is a watershed in the emergence of party caucuses, corresponding committees, and various other meetings resembling more closely much more fully-formed political parties, parties now using the labels Federalists and Republicans.[48] "Everywhere, though in varying degrees, party machinery was organized more efficiently," Morton Borden tells us in 1967's *Parties and Politics in the Early Republic, 1789–1815.*[49] "Rather remarkable transformations had taken

---

45 *Gazette of the United States* Wednesday, March 13, 1793, 3.

46 "The Republicans made it perfectly clear that if they should ever get the upper hand in Congress, they would make short work of [Treasury Secretary] Hamilton," Ralph Volney Harlow tells us. "When the Congressional elections of 1792 assured them of a clear majority in the next House, they settled back to wait for better days, openly announcing their intentions of blocking further Federalist action by every means in their power," Harlow says. "When the third Congress convened, the Republicans with all the seriousness of reformers with a mission settled down to their self-appointed task of restoring the Constitutional balance." Ralph Volney Harlow, *The History of Legislative Methods in the Period before 1825.* Yale University Press, 1917, 151–152.

47 "Washington would start his second term with a hostile Republican majority in the lower house," Wilfred E. Binkley tells us. "Even before the new Congress was seated, the emboldened Republicans in the House started the campaign against [Treasury Secretary] Hamilton that was in time to drive him into private life," Binkley says. Wilfred E. Binkley, *The Powers of the President: Problems of American Democracy.* Doubleday, Doran and Company, 1937, 36.

48 "A closer concert was developing among...the Federal establishment and the Republican interest, and people of like mind in the states," Roy F. Nichols tells us. "The opposition Congressmen were seeking to arouse sentiment and gain support in their constituencies. They were writing back home to the local elites or courthouse associates and stimulating them to persuade others to hold meetings, to pass resolutions." "Likewise," Nichols explains, "they communicated with the legislative leaders at home, attempting to influence them to provide official state pronouncements to be sent to Senators and Congressmen to demonstrate either the strength of the opposition to the establishment or popular support of its measures." Roy F. Nichols, *The Invention of the American Political Parties.* The Macmillan Company, 1967, 190.

49 Morton Borden, *Parties and Politics in the Early Republic, 1789–1815.* Thomas Y. Crowell Company, 1967, 54.

place in political attitudes and practices since the inception of the Constitution a decade before," Borden says. "Campaigning, which once had been denounced as improper, increased to such an extent that it became socially acceptable in most regions." Caucuses, corresponding committees, and even conventions in some states wielded influence over the campaigning of the day as politics came out-of-doors and into the public in a way unlike any time yet. "Tickets became common and voters were advised to consider the good of the party as superior to the personal characteristics of a candidate," Borden points out. "More people actively participated in politics than ever before and were urged to do so by local leaders." Letters, meetings, pamphlets, speeches, and even cartoons and decorative items all took hold in 1794's midterm contests for the fourth Congress. Republicans kept their House majority with a 59 – 47 margin in the fourth Congress, while the Federalists held on to their majority in the Senate.

"The war will soon begin again," Rep. Ames told Thomas Dwight on Thursday, May 19, 1796 of that coming Fall's presidential race. "Who shall be President and Vice, are questions that will put an end to the armed neutrality of parties," Ames wrote months before President Washington made his much-anticipated announcement of his decision not to run for a third term in office. "Mr. Adams will be our man, and Jefferson theirs. Faction will send its recruiting sergeants round to obtain recruits for Jefferson," Ames said. "The choice of electors will be attended to everywhere with eagle eyes," Ames anticipated accurately of the 1796 election.[50]

President Washington's letter of Monday, September 19, 1796 announcing his decision not to run for a third term, the ensuing candidacies of then-Vice President John Adams and Thomas Jefferson that November 1796, and that fall's Congressional clashes delivering Federalist majorities in the House and the Senate all were hallmarks of a more fully-formed partisanship still seen as undesirable and unnecessary by some public figures, not least of which was the departing President. Washington's farewell letter spoke to his fears of the divisions of partisanship in the capitol he was leaving.[51] Weary of the rifts in his own cabinet and in Congress and wary of the partisan currents in the newspapers of the day, President Washington went through draft after draft of his departing letter. Alexander Hamilton's assistance in drafting passages in the President's letter took close aim at the nation's political parties that the former Treasury Secretary himself had been so

---

50 Fisher Ames to Thomas Dwight, Thursday, May 19, 1796, in *Works of Fisher Ames with a Selection from his Speeches and Correspondence, Volume I*, ed. Seth Ames. Little, Brown and Company, 1854, 193 – 194.

51 *Farewell Address, Monday, September 19, 1796*, in *The Papers of George Washington, Volume XX, 1 April – 21 September 1796*, eds. Jennifer E. Steenshorne, David R. Hoth, William F. Ferraro, Thomas E. Dulan, and Benjamin L. Huggins. The University Press of Virginia, 2019, 703 – 718.

pivotal a figure in polarizing and steering behind-the-scenes. Eliminating a passage sharply critical of the newspapers of the day, the nation's Federalists and Republicans won no such reprieve, and were subject to some of President Washington's sharpest words in his September 1796 letter.

"The Sage of Monticello and the Sage of Quincy sat out the event in bucolic retirement, while their parties ran the race for them," William Nisbet Chambers' *Political Parties in a New Nation: The American Experience, 1776 – 1809* tells us of the 1796 presidential contest.[52] No map in the history of America's elections is perhaps as astonishing as 1796's contest between the Sage of Monticello and the Sage of Quincy – the fully-formed Federalists and Republicans repudiating the denunciations of the dangers of partisanship by President Washington in a sharp and stark geographic and regional division between the Federalists in New England and the Republicans in the Mid-Atlantic and the South. People in all parts of the country threw themselves headfirst into the contest of the Federalists and the Republicans as the departing President urged his fellow Americans to do just the opposite, with political parties in defiance of a President leaving office themselves leaving their own indelible and undeniable mark in the last election of the eighteenth century.

---

52 William Nisbet Chambers, *Political Parties in a New Nation: The American Experience, 1776 – 1809.* Oxford University Press, 1963, 114.

Chapter 2 Federalists, Democratic Republicans, and the Emergence of the Democratic Party, 1801–1853

"We are all Republicans. We are all Federalists." Spoken in the newly built Capitol building of a national capital still taking shape on the banks of the Potomac River, President Thomas Jefferson's words delivered for his Inaugural on Wednesday, March 4, 1801 mark a formative moment in an enduring two-party history, the names of our Democrats and Republicans still tracing back today to the Jeffersonian era of the Democratic Republicans.

"The name [Republican] remained as the label practically every man in politics assumed," William Nisbet Chambers tells us of the early years of the nineteenth century in his 1963 *Political Parties in a New Nation: The American Experience, 1776–1809*.[53] However, at the national level by the mid-1820s, in Chambers' memorable description, the country saw the collapse of the "once stately Republican mansion." For all intents and purposes, the Democratic Republican ticket and name had ceased to exist by the end of President James Monroe's administration. The "Republican mansion" scattered to the winds in the scramble of candidates running to succeed Monroe in 1824's presidential election. Still, supporters of Andrew Jackson later claimed at least part of that popular banner in the name of their Democratic ticket for Jackson's supporters in the mid-1830s. The other part of the once-popular Jeffersonian banner took hold temporarily in the National Republicans as a name for Jackson's opponents who campaigned against him in his reelection in 1832. Jackson's foes kept the Republican name alive and carried it forward until the emergence of the Whig ticket in Jackson's second term.

Though the Federalists never again won a presidential election after Jefferson's 1800 rout of John Adams, they still held on for years in Congress with seats in the House and Senate as an out-of-step opposition party through a succession of Democratic Republican administrations. Federalist candidates regularly won a scattering of seats in the House and Senate, mostly in the Mid-Atlantic states and in New England. Their deep roots there kept them in Governors Mansions and state legislatures, but the Federalist banner eventually ended with the last Federalist presidential ticket in Rufus King's 1816 candidacy against Democratic Republican James Monroe.

---

53 William Nisbet Chambers, *Political Parties in a New Nation: The American Experience, 1776–1809*. Oxford University Press, 1963, 200.

https://doi.org/10.1515/9783111340029-003

Having spent the weeks before President-elect Jefferson's Inaugural naming appointees to vacancies in the final days of his term, President John Adams left his fellow Federalists in disarray. Following weeks of last-minute appointments hurriedly sent to the Senate to be confirmed by the lame-duck Congress, "the last mad [acts] of a mad administration," Georgia's then-Senator James Jackson told then-Secretary of State James Madison in May 1801, Adams left the capital for his home in Massachusetts before dawn on the day of Jefferson's Inaugural.[54] "As he rode away from the unkempt capital village," William Nisbet Chambers tells us of Adams' early-morning departure, "the era of supremacy for the Federalist Party vanished with him."[55] Years later, the Democratic Republicans reminded their supporters of Adams' lame-duck appointments, a lasting and long-remembered legacy of the Federalists.

Jefferson's election by the lame-duck House in February 1801 was the artifact of an improbable set of circumstances that led to an Electoral College tie with his running mate, Aaron Burr.[56] Infamous as Burr's name is in the annals of American history for his association with various and sundry schemes, his part in 1800's electoral stalemate with Jefferson is far from his most egregious act. The actual circumstances of 1801's election in the House offer less of Burr's manipulative machinations and more of the mischief of the Federalists in a week's delaying of the selection of Jefferson to sew confusion and embarrass the President-elect.[57] Jefferson's Federalist foes prolonged his election in the House as one of the more misguided instances of political mischief in American history, an ill-thought strategy mostly intended to embarrass Jefferson that misjudged the moment and only served to frustrate Americans still further with the faltering Federalists.

With the country's lawmakers and the public in the early nineteenth century seemingly more accepting of the idea of political parties, the Twelfth Amendment established a Constitutional place for party tickets in presidential elections. Ratified as a corrective to the workings of Article II, Section 1 of the Constitution that had allowed for the tie of Jefferson and Burr in 1800, the Twelfth Amendment effectively marked the permanent place of party tickets for the President and Vice

---

54 James Jackson to James Madison, Friday, May 15, 1801, in *The Papers of James Madison, Secretary of State Series, Volume I, 4 March-31 July 1801*, eds. Robert J. Brugger, Robert Rhodes Crout, Dru Dowdy, Robert A. Rutland, and Jeanne K. Sisson. The University Press of Virginia, 1986, 176.

55 William Nisbet Chambers, *Political Parties in a New Nation: The American Experience, 1776–1809.* Oxford University Press, 1963, 169.

56 Electing Jefferson after 35 ballots in the House on Tuesday, February 17, 1801, the lame duck House session of the 6th Congress adjourned on Tuesday, March 3, 1801.

57 Milton Lomask, *Aaron Burr: The Years from Princeton to Vice President, 1756–1805.* Farrar Straus Giroux, 1979, 277.

President.[58] Hereafter, Presidents and Vice Presidents ran together as a ticket for the same Electoral votes. Considerations of geography and of balancing different constituencies in selecting a party ticket replaced the complicated stratagems of what had been essentially distinct candidacies for President and Vice President before the Twelfth Amendment's ratification, with the ever-present possibility of mishaps or of a tie-vote of candidates on the same ticket, as had happened in 1800's race.

In the early years of the nineteenth century, especially after the Twelfth Amendment's ratification, Democratic Republicans and Federalists worked to create balanced, national tickets in presidential elections. Tickets of the President and Vice President began to look to geographical balance in the selection of nominees and their running-mates. Jefferson and his Democratic Republicans looked to New England to bring some balance to their Virginia-led tickets. Whatever their struggles and stumbles, Federalists still succeeded in securing their own geographic balance. Federalist Charles C. Pinckney's bid for President in November 1804 brought regional balance to the Federalist ticket as the South Carolina presidential nominee was balanced by the selection of his running-mate, Rufus King of New York. In November 1808, when South Carolina's Pinckney ran for a second time for President on the Federalist ticket, New York's King once again stood as Pinckney's Vice-Presidential running mate. It became commonplace in the decades to come for party tickets to look to geography, as evident in President James Madison's selection of Elbridge Gerry of Massachusetts as his running mate in 1812. James Monroe's running mate in 1816 and in 1820, Daniel Tompkins of New York, was not an especially distinguished figure, but brought regional balance of New England to another Virginia presidential ticket.

The expansion of the country with new states and the Westward migration under Jefferson's administration set the Democratic Republicans and Federalists at odds, and it left the Federalists out of step yet again with the large number of Americans moving westward in the early nineteenth century. Settlers moving their families across the Allegheny Mountains into the Ohio River Valley and

---

58 In a time when the Federalists found themselves fighting to return as a popular party in the public mind, some of that party's leaders opposed the Twelfth Amendment and later embraced a Constitutional Amendment limiting the President to one four-year term. Some Federalists also backed an Amendment limiting the residency of the Presidency so that no state could be the residence of successive Presidents. "A thrust at the Virginia Dynasty was implicit," Wilfred E. Binkley tells us in an Amendment backed by Federalists, "that 'the same person shall not be elected President of the United States a second time nor shall the President be elected from the same state two terms in succession.'" Wilfred E. Binkley, *American Political Parties: Their Natural History* Alfred A. Knopf, 1943, 96.

still further westward into the Mississippi River Valley faced Federalist objections to calls for statehood for Ohio, Tennessee, and other states.[59] Democratic Republicans and Federalists fought heated legislative brawls over the admission and statehood of Kentucky, Ohio, Tennessee, and other states, with Federalists often casting the only votes against admission of these states and objecting to these efforts for territorial expansion in the West.[60] The push of more Americans into the West, then, pushed the Federalists away from the American people still further.

Nationally, parties in the early years of the nineteenth century were needed to shape and steer the messages of candidates and the mobilization of their supporters during elections, especially as new states entered the union and as some of these new states saw their newly-enacted state Constitutions opening the franchise to larger groups of voters. Voting in many states was wholly the work of the political parties, not just in the leaflets, pamphlets, and other printed materials of candidates, but in the very ballots used in almost all parts of the country for most of the nineteenth century's elections. Until the end of the nineteenth century, ballots in the United States were the pure product of the political parties. Their replacement by state-printed, standardized ballots at the end of the nineteenth century came at long last only in response to controversies of election fraud in the years after the Civil War.

In the early years of the nineteenth century, Democratic Republicans, Federalists, and later Whigs carefully tended to their party newspapers and to cultivating and supporting the sympathetic editors whose commentary and coverage of their campaigns helped to strengthen and to sustain their supporters. In most cities and towns across the country in the early years of the nineteenth century, most newspapers and their editors aligned themselves with the party tickets, their very titles sometimes incorporating the names Democratic, Republican and Whig in newspapers like *The Nashville Whig and Tennessee Advertiser, The National Whig, The Whig Standard, The Missouri Whig, The Ohio Democrat, The National Republican, The New Orleans Republican*, and so many others. Sometimes, the most effective and loyal editors were also rewarded after successful elections with either government printing contracts or much-sought appointments to government posts.

Without a unifying national leader, the Federalists in the early years of the nineteenth century dwindled mostly to a scattering of House seats, state legislative chambers, and local offices in New England and across parts of the Mid-Atlantic. Alexander Hamilton's fatal duel with then-Vice President Aaron Burr in July

---

59 Robert V. Remini, *The Revolutionary Age of Andrew Jackson.* Harper and Row Publishers, 1976, 5.
60 Michael Allen, "The Federalists and the West, 1783–1803." *The Western Pennsylvania Historical Magazine* 61, no. 4, October 1978, 324, 330.

1804 and the disorganization it left in the Federalist ranks left the once-vibrant party adrift. In November 1804's election, Republicans held 114 seats in the House and 27 in the Senate to only 28 Federalists in the House and just 7 Federalists in the Senate. Jefferson easily dispatched the Federalists in winning reelection to his second term in 1804. 1808's presidential election – with James Madison now at the top of the national ticket – saw the Democratic Republicans easily defeat Federalist presidential candidate Charles C. Pinckney, who was unable for a second consecutive election as a candidate of the Federalists to even carry his home state of South Carolina.

President Thomas Jefferson and his fellow Virginians James Madison and James Monroe led the Democratic Republicans to establish their roots in most parts of the country in the early years of the nineteenth century, especially in the South and in the newly settled states further to the west. New York always remained a reliable Democratic Republican state thanks to the work of the Virginians in cultivating allies there for years like George Clinton, Daniel Tompkins, and others. As an out-of-step opposition, Federalists never came close to winning a presidential election again. President Monroe's unchallenged bid for reelection to a second term in 1820 left the Federalists barely holding anything with only a scattering of offices in New England and a handful of districts in Maryland and Virginia.

"Jefferson and Madison recognized and adhered to the political party that elected them, and they left it united and powerful. The first year of Mr. Monroe's second term had scarcely passed away before the political atmosphere became inflamed to an unprecedented extent," one of the most careful observers of the Democratic Republicans in the 1820s, Martin Van Buren, wrote in his *Inquiry into the Origin and Course of Political Parties in the United States.* Van Buren wrote this of the years just after 1820's re-election of Monroe, a time of the crumbling of the "Republican mansion" improbably following on the heels of the Federalists' collapse. "The Republican Party, so long in the ascendant, and apparently so omnipotent, was literally shattered into fragments, and we had no fewer than five Republican Presidential candidates in the field," Van Buren observed of Monroe's second-term in the run-up to 1824's presidential election. "These [candidates] having few higher motives for the selection of their candidates or stronger incentives to action than individual preferences or antipathies, moved the bitter waters of political agitation to their lowest depths," Van Buren said of the rivalries that marked the fracturing of the long-dominant Democratic Republicans in the presidential election of 1824.[61]

---

61 Martin Van Buren, *Inquiry into the Origin and Course of Political Parties in the United States.* Hurd and Houghton, 1867, 3–4.

1824's presidential contest, the first to be decided in the House since the Twelfth Amendment's ratification, saw the three candidates – then-Sen. Andrew Jackson, then-Secretary of State John Quincy Adams, and then-Treasury Secretary William Crawford – faced each other in the lame-duck House, after dividing the country's Electoral votes in an election of geographical and regional candidacies that had included then-Speaker of the House Henry Clay and, for a time, South Carolina's John Calhoun, as the "five Republican Presidential candidates" Van Buren had written about in his *Inquiry into the Origins and Course of Political Parties in the United States.*[62] For only the second time in the country's history, the House would select the President under the new procedures of the Twelfth Amendment.

With John Quincy Adams' selection as President by the House on Wednesday, February 9, 1825 and with the new President's selection of Henry Clay as his Secretary of State not even a week later on Monday, February 14, 1825, Andrew Jackson's supporters threw themselves headlong into beginning the building of what is today the Democratic Party. In the absence of evidence of collusion between John Quincy Adams and Henry Clay to thwart Jackson, the ill-considered selection of Clay by Adams as his nominee for Secretary of State was all the proof needed by a now-embittered Jackson and his supporters to believe the allegations of collusion in a Corrupt Bargain between Adams and Clay.[63] Jackson's supporters spoke loudly of the theft of the Presidency by Adams and Clay with an anger unlike anything seen to date in America's presidential elections. They convened meetings and gatherings in every corner of the country, held caucuses in state legislatures, and circulated all manner of correspondence to make the most of every accusation and allegation of back-room, closed-door deals of Adams and Clay in Washington, all to burnish the reputation and build support for Jackson for his rematch with Adams in 1828.

---

62 "Each man," William Nisbet Chambers explains, "drew what elements he could around him, on a personal basis, in terms of more or less contrived conjunctions of interests, or on sectional grounds." William Nisbet Chambers, *Political Parties in a New Nation: The American Experience, 1776–1809.* Oxford University Press, 1963, 201.

63 As the most attentive and careful historian of this time, Robert V. Remini does little to disabuse history of the fallout from Clay's acceptance of his nomination by Adams. "Within 3 days of his Inauguration, John Quincy Adams had performed the stupendous feat of creating an opposition bent on destroying his Administration and denying him, like his father, a second term in office." Robert V. Remini, *The Election of Andrew Jackson.* J.B. Lippincott Company, 1963, 28. The misjudgment compounded itself with each denial, Remini says. "Naturally stories circulated that Clay had sold out to Adams in return for the State Department, but this Clay angrily denied and he expended so much energy in his denial that it was almost impossible to believe him." Robert V. Remini, *Andrew Jackson.* Twayne Publishers, 1996, 96.

As 1828's election grew closer, the work of Martin Van Buren proved to be of no small importance to Jackson. Van Buren's travels and meetings with the leaders of the Democratic Republicans in Georgia, North Carolina, South Carolina, and Virginia helped pave the way for Jackson's 1828 ticket, and helped to build what was soon to become the Democratic Party.[64] "Van Buren is now the great electioneering manager for General Jackson, as he was before the last election for Mr. Crawford," President John Quincy Adams wrote on Saturday, May 12, 1827. "He is now acting over the part in the affairs of the Union which Aaron Burr performed in 1799 and 1800, and there is much resemblance of character, manners, and even person, between the two men," Adams said of Van Buren.[65] Van Buren's travel and his correspondence with pro-Jackson caucuses in state legislatures and in meetings of all manner took the first steps toward building what was to eventually become the Democratic Party.

Symbols of Jackson's resoluteness – the oak tree, the hickory broom – became popular with Jackson's supporters as they laid the groundwork for his 1828 race. Hickory Clubs were organized in many parts of the country. Hurrah Boys – Jackson's name for the young men who filled the ranks of his supporters in the small towns and the crossroads settlements across the country – handed out flyers, handbills, and writings of all kinds to tell Jackson's story.[66] The alleged Corrupt Bargain in 1825 to thwart Jackson's election became a popular rallying cry, one kept front and center by the loyalists preparing for Jackson's second bid for the Presidency.

"JACKSON FOREVER, THE HERO OF TWO WARS AND OF ORLEANS!" one of the most famous handbills from 1828's contest proclaimed of Jackson as the popular sentiments stoked nonstop for almost four years brought an enthusiasm and an excitement to 1828's election. "THE MAN OF THE PEOPLE, HE WHO COULD NOT BARTER NOR BARGAIN FOR THE PRESIDENCY!" this same handbill promised. Jackson rode a populist wave all the way to his 1828 rout of President John Quincy Adams.[67] When Jackson's steamboat, *Pennsylvania*, carried the President-elect on the Cumberland River and then the Ohio River in the first leg of his journey to the nation's capital, *Pennsylvania*'s crew had two hickory brooms affixed to the bow of their boat.

---

64 Robert V. Remini, *Martin Van Buren and the Making of the Democratic Party.* Columbia University Press, 1959, 124.

65 John Quincy Adams, *Memoirs of John Quincy Adams, Comprising Portions of His Diary from 1795 to 1848, Volume 7,* ed. Charles Francis Adams. J.B. Lippincott and Company, 1875, 272.

66 Lynn Hudson Parsons, *The Birth of Modern Politics: Andrew Jackson, John Quincy Adams, and the Election of 1828.* Oxford University Press, 2009.

67 Robert V. Remini, *The Jackson Era.* Harlan Davidson, Inc. 1989, xii.

The death of President-elect Jackson's wife in December 1828 compounded the ill-will between the defeated President Adams and President-elect Jackson, lingering in the anger felt by the President-elect for the grief he believed Adams and his supporters' words against him had caused his late wife during her illness. Slighted by Jackson's unwillingness to visit him at the White House days after the President-elect's arrival in Washington, Adams faced the decision of whether to attend the Capitol ceremony swearing in the new President. Finally, just days before the ceremony, Adams decided not to attend the Inauguration. Instead, Adams and his family left the Executive Mansion and traveled to a nearby home on Meridian Hill in Washington where they spent the night while revelers welcomed Jackson to his new home in their celebration on the lawn and grounds of the Executive Mansion.[68] Adams and his family lived for several months at Meridian Hill before their return to the family home in Massachusetts.

President Jackson's first term brought his opponents together temporarily under the banner of National Republicanism, including Kentucky Senator Henry Clay and Massachusetts Senator Daniel Webster. Clay, Webster, and the anti-Jackson opposition took to calling their ticket the National Republicans, a callback and nod to the Democratic Republicans of years earlier. Jackson faced little real challenge in his reelection in 1832, easily dispatching the National Republican ticket of Henry Clay and his Vice-Presidential running mate, John Sergeant. What remains a lasting legacy of 1832's election to this day are the national conventions that still dominate presidential elections for the Democrats and Republicans.

With little in comparison to the large and loud national gatherings they soon became, party nominating conventions burst on the scene for the first time in 1832's election both for President Andrew Jackson's supporters and for the anti-Jackson National Republicans. December 1831's National Republican Convention in Baltimore saw some 175 anti-Jackson delegates from 18 states assemble to select their national ticket of Henry Clay and John Sergeant.[69] Months later, Monday, May 21, 1832's gaveling into session of the first national convention of President Andrew Jackson's supporters, calling themselves at the time Republicans, also met in Baltimore. President Jackson's convention had some 320 pro-Jackson delegates from every state except Missouri, whose delegates were delayed by travel difficulties.[70] Jackson's supporters assembled to nominate the President to his second term and

---

68 Samuel Flagg Bemis, *John Quincy Adams and the Union*. Alfred A. Knopf, 1956, 154.

69 James S. Chase, *Emergence of the Presidential Nominating Convention, 1789–1832*. The University of Illinois Press, 1973, 216.

70 James S. Chase, *Emergence of the Presidential Nominating Convention, 1789–1832*. The University of Illinois Press, 1973, 263.

to nominate Martin Van Burn as Jackson's running mate.[71] Adopting a rule requiring a super-majority of delegates for the nomination of the ticket, May 1832's convention is remembered for establishing one of the more far-reaching rules of any political party in the history of the United States, specifically the requirement for two-thirds of convention delegates for nomination of the President that lasted in the Democratic Party until June 1936's Democratic National Convention. It left the party in adjournment in at least one decisive and divisive convention in the party's history in April 1860 in Charleston, South Carolina, when then-Senator Stephen A. Douglas held a majority of Democratic delegates but fell short of the two-thirds needed to head the ticket. The rule later embarrassed the party in the first national convention of the era of coast-to-coast radio broadcasts in July 1924 at the Democratic convention in New York City's Madison Square Garden.

Senator Henry Clay's storied Monday, April 14, 1834 speech on the Senate floor rallying opponents of President Jackson in his second term begins the history of the Whig Party for the next two decades as one of the most important political parties in American history, a party largely absorbed into the Republican Party almost exactly 20 years after Clay's speech launched the Whigs. Whigs became the banner for the anti-Democratic opposition stretching across the next two decades until the eve of the Civil War.[72] The Whig ticket held together the anti-Jackson opposition nationally, including some of the first stirrings of anti-slavery sentiments for a growing number of Whigs as the first such movement in any major national party in the history of the United States.

The Whigs are remembered almost as a kind of cultural melting pot in the mid-nineteenth century, a big-tent bringing together an assemblage of personalities, factions, and interests whose debates and disagreements shaped America's political life and its campaigning in presidential elections long after the Whigs' disappearance in the mid-1850s. The newly-formed Whigs saw their first candidates elected to seats in the House in 1836, with 100 or so Whigs from the newly-formed party elected to the House at a time when that chamber was led by a 128-seat Democratic majority.[73] 1836's presidential election saw the Whigs stumble somewhat in seeing no fewer than three different Whig candidates divide its vote for President in 1836, including Ohio Whig William Henry Harrison and Massachusetts Whig

71 Robert V. Remini, *The Revolutionary Age of Andrew Jackson.* Harper and Row Publishers, 1976, 143.

72 Michael F. Holt, *The Rise and Fall of the American Whig Party: Jacksonian Politics and the Onset of the Civil War.* Oxford University Press, 1999, 36–37.

73 Kenneth C. Martis, *The Historical Atlas of the Political Parties in the United States Congress, 1789–1989.* Macmillan Publishing Company, 1989, 94.

Chapter 2 Federalists, Democratic Republicans, and the Democratic Party, 1801–1853 —— **29**

Daniel Webster, easing the way for Martin Van Buren to hold the White House for the Democrats.

From its first Congressional candidates elected in 1836 through its ill-fated final nominating convention in June 1852 where it turned away Whig President Millard Fillmore's nomination to run for a second term, the Whigs seemed always to be a balancing act of different constituencies, seeking to hold together a patchwork party that always lacked a center yet never lacked for colorful and contentious coalitions of interests and larger-than-life personalities. Whigs were always a house divided, welcoming the opponents of President Andrew Jackson and whatever foes of Jackson's successor, Martin Van Buren, happened to find their place under the Whig tent. Balancing its many differences always remained the difficult work of the Whigs. Its assortment of so many different interests and rival personalities so loosely tethered together at such an important time in the nation's history is still remembered to this day as both a strength and a weakness for the Whig Party. Whigs sometimes favored tariffs and fought for protective measures for domestic manufacturers in their presidential platforms and at their national conventions. Other Whigs opposed tariffs and fought just as fiercely against them. Whigs sometimes favored investment by the government in much-needed internal improvements. Other Whigs warned of the encroachment of such investments. Anti-slavery Whigs – sometimes called Conscience Whigs – spoke out against the slave states and their hold on the Democrats. The anti-slavery Whigs are remembered to this day as the first major presence of an anti-slavery constituency ever in any national political party. Against the anti-slavery sentiment in the Whig Party were pro-slavery Whigs who defended slavery and supported the anti-abolitionists violently surging across many parts of the country at the end of the 1830s and the early 1840s.

1840's election of William Henry Harrison – a candidate who'd run as one of three Whigs for President in 1836's election – is remembered to this day as the first of two Whig presidential candidates to win the White House. Elected in a campaign filled with symbolic appeals by the Whigs to the rustic imagery of log cabins and hard cider, Harrison's defeat of President Martin Van Buren delivered, too, the first Whig majorities in the House of Representatives and the Senate. Defeating President Martin Van Buren, the third sitting President in the nation's history to lose in running for reelection, the Whigs dealt the Democrats a decisive defeat by a political party not even a decade old. From 1840 until 1852 when the last Whig ticket ran in the loss of Whig Winfield Scott to Democrat Franklin Pierce, Democrats and Whigs fought close-to-the-wire national campaigns that brought unprecedented levels of voter enthusiasm and turnout in most states.

For all of their differences and their disagreements within their party, Whig tickets in the 1840s and the early 1850s were always helped by support from some of the most prominent newspapers of the day, whose sympathetic editors and reporters rallied readers to Whig tickets. Whigs won the support of some of the most respected editors of the day, including Horace Greeley's *The New York Tribune* and Henry Raymond's *The New York Daily Times*. *The New York Daily Times'* Raymond and *The New York Tribune's* Greeley years later helped to build up the Republicans after the decline of the Whigs in the mid-1850s.

With the experience of the Whigs in the early 1840s in establishing themselves as a loud and lively opposition to the Democrats, Whigs still faced an always-precarious place in the nation's political life, including the death of the two Presidents elected by the Whigs and the succession of Vice Presidents into office whose unpopularity foretold the fractures that eventually finished the Whigs nationally. Already weakened by the tragedies in the death of Whig President William Henry Harrison in 1841 and the death of Whig President Zachary Taylor in 1850, Whig fates worsened with the faltering of their two Vice Presidential successors, Whig Vice President-turned-President John Tyler (Tyler Too to the late William Henry Harrison's Tippecanoe) and Whig Vice President-turned-President Millard Fillmore. When President Tyler and later President Fillmore abandoned some of the platforms and positions of their predecessors popular with their fellow Whigs, it further fractured the party. Whig national conventions were the first nominating conventions ever to reject their own sitting Presidents. President Tyler was struck from the Whig ticket at May 1844's national convention, and President Fillmore was replaced on the presidential ticket by his own Whig party at its June 1852 convention.

Tuesday, April 6, 1841's swearing-in of Whig President John Tyler as the first Vice President to follow the death of a President began a fraught moment for the Whigs during what would otherwise have been a moment of celebration for Whigs after winning their first presidential contest only a few months earlier. Instead, Whigs in Congress led by Senator Henry Clay led the opposition to their own President. As President Tyler vetoed tariff measures and other bills favored by Senator Clay and his fellow Whigs, opponents in the President's own party grew. When Tyler sought to fill vacancies in his cabinet following the resignations of cabinet members who'd been appointed by the late President Harrison, Whig Senators blocked their confirmations. Defeats of several of Tyler's cabinet nominees, the defeat of Justices nominated by Tyler to the Supreme Court, and the first veto override in history and even calls for Tyler's impeachment by the House expressed the depths of Whig unhappiness with their own President.

When May 1844's Whig national convention in Baltimore wrote a new chapter in the history of America's political parties in rejecting for the first time the sitting President from their national ticket, it marked a watershed moment for the Whigs and their rival Democrats in elevating the importance of national nominating conventions. President John Tyler is the first of four sitting Presidents to have their national convention deny them the nomination to run for a second term, a place in history shared with Whig President Millard Fillmore, Democratic President Franklin Pierce, and Republican President Chester A. Arthur.

November 1844's contest between Democratic nominee James Polk and Whig founder Henry Clay is a decisive moment in the nineteenth century's political parties, as Whigs and Democrats faced off in as well-organized of a contest as ever in the fight for the Presidency. The election had already shattered precedent for Presidents in May 1844 when the Whig convention struck President John Tyler from the ticket and replaced him with the venerable Henry Clay, and it spoke to a fall campaign between the Democrats and the Whigs like no other before. Never had America's political parties been so well-organized in a presidential election over such an extensive electorate, a far cry from President James Monroe's unchallenged bid for reelection to a second term in 1820 just a few years earlier. In 1844's election, Democrats and Whigs were like two opposing armies, with well-organized groups of state and local loyalists taking the campaigns of Polk and Clay into every city and town, making it one of the closest elections ever in the history of the United States, decided by just a few thousand votes carried narrowly in New York by Polk.[74]

With Democrat James Polk's election in 1844, one of the great clashes in the history of the Democratic and Whig rivalry was settled for the moment, but the Whigs rebounded to win their last House majority in 1846's midterms. Elected for just one two-year term in the House for Illinois' seventh House District in this election, Rep. Abraham Lincoln was the only Whig House member of Congress from the Democratic stronghold of Illinois. Lincoln spent his two-years in the Capitol as a part of the last Whig House majority in the party's history, returning to his home in Illinois where he remained a steadfast Whig until its last days as a party.

With President James Polk's pledge to serve only one four-year term if elected President, 1848's election became a historic opening and opportunity for the Democrats and Whigs to face each other in one of the last major national clashes of the two parties. Slaveowner and retired General Zachary Taylor's nomination divided

---

74 1844 is the first of six "hairbreadth" elections, using Neal R. Peirce's term for elections in the history of presidential elections decided by just 1 state, sometimes by just a few thousand votes. These elections – 1844, 1880, 1884, 1888, 1916, and 2000 – all came down to just 1 state, and in 4 of the states (with the exceptions of California in 1916 and Florida in 2000), the election came down to New York. In 1844's contest, Polk carried New York by a mere 2,500 or so votes, Peirce says, out of more than 470,000 votes cast in the state, one of the closest margins of any election in the country's history. Neal R. Peirce, *The People's President: The Electoral College in American History and the Direct Vote Alternative.* Simon and Schuster, 1968, 318.

the Whigs, with a large number of Whigs backing Taylor's nomination at that moment when anti-slavery Whigs found themselves growing in number. Taylor was the second Whig elected President – and was the second Whig President to die while in office.[75] Vice President Millard Fillmore became that party's second sitting President to subsequently face removal from the Whig ticket. June 1852's Whig National Convention was a drawn-out, bitterly-fought convention, a fight taking 53 ballots by delegates at the convention and almost a week's tallies of votes by delegates to finally reject President Fillmore, replacing the sitting Whig President on the national ticket with General Winfield Scott. For the second time, the Whigs had forced a sitting Whig President off of the national ticket, and as the Whigs collapsed after Scott's defeat in 1852, so came to an end one of the most important political parties in the history of the United States.

One of those Whigs finding himself uncertain about his own future in a world without the Whigs was Illinois' Abraham Lincoln. "I think I am a Whig, but others say there are no Whigs," Lincoln confided to his friend, Joshua Speed, in August 1855, at a time when little if anything was left of the Whigs. A number had found themselves taking part the first Republican meetings and state conventions sweeping across parts of Iowa, Michigan, Wisconsin, and even Lincoln's home state of Illinois a year earlier.[76] Lincoln was one of many Whigs whose loyalty to the Whigs was not easily replaced.[77] It took almost another year for Lincoln to finally cast his fortunes with the Republican Party, such were the attachments of Lincoln and so many other Whigs to their party.

By Tuesday, November 7, 1854's midterms, the remnants of what was left of the Whigs was just one of what was now a scattering of smaller parties that took the

---

75 Whig Zachary Taylor was the first President elected with opposition majorities in the House and the Senate – with a 113–108 Democratic House and a 35–25 Democratic Senate elected in Tuesday, November 7, 1848's election. Kenneth C. Martis, *The Historical Atlas of the Political Parties in the United States Congress, 1789–1989.* Macmillan Publishing Company, 1989, 103. Republican Richard M. Nixon and Republican George H.W. Bush would be the only other newly-elected Presidents in history without their own parties in either the House or the Senate.

76 Abraham Lincoln to Joshua F. Speed, Friday, August 24, 1855, in *The Collected Works of Abraham Lincoln, Volume II*, ed. Roy P. Basler. Rutgers University Press, 1953, 322–323.

77 "[Abraham Lincoln] found it hard to abandon [the Whig Party]," Richard Hofstadter tells us in 1948's *The American Political Tradition and the Men Who Made It.* "For two years after the Republicans had formed state and local state organizations, he refused to join them, and even while supporting their candidate [John C.] Fremont, in 1856, he carefully avoided speaking of himself as [a Republican]. In the fall of 1854, hungering for the Senatorial nomination and fearing to offend numerous old-line Whigs in Illinois, he fled Springfield...to avoid attending [an October 1854] Republican state convention there." Richard Hofstadter, *The American Political Tradition and the Men Who Made It.* Alfred A. Knopf, 1948, 97.

country to an unprecedented chapter in the history of America's political parties. American, American Republican, American Whig, Anti-Know Nothing Democrat, Anti-Know Nothing Independent, Anti-Know Nothing Whig, Anti-Nebraska, Anti-Nebraska Democrat, Anti-Slavery Whig, Buchanan Democrat, Fillmore American, Free Soil, Free Soil Democrat, Fusion, Independent Democrat, Independent Whig, Know Nothing, Know Nothing Democrat, Know Nothing Whig, Native American, Nebraska Democrat, Temperance, Union, Union Whig, and Whig were some of the 44 or more tickets that represented lawmakers running for seats in 1854.[78] When the dust finally settled from tabulations and tallies across the country, 1854's midterms were like nothing ever seen before.

1854's midterms were an election like no other, with perhaps fewer than 40 House members in all having any affiliation with what was left of the Whigs. One of the largest blocks of House members, some 50 or so in all, were in the anti-Catholic, anti-immigrant American Party.[79] Another 80 or so House members were Democrats, but the largest block of House members had such a loosely designated scattering of different names and tickets that their they became known simply as the Opposition, a block of House members numbering some 100 or so members.

"*The Congressional Globe*," the late Joel H. Silbey tells us of this unusual chapter in the convening of thirty-fourth Congress in March 1855, "did not list the party identification of members at the opening of the session as it usually did."[80] Instead, the patchwork of officeholders in the House chamber coalesced together into a coalition comprised of the Opposition members and some 50 or so American members of the House.[81] In every Congress from the first Congress in 1789 through 1855, the House and Senate chambers had always had a single, clear party to form a two-year majority. In every Congress since 1855, the House and Senate chambers have

---

78 Kenneth C. Martis, *The Historical Atlas of the Political Parties in the United States Congress, 1789–1989.* Macmillan Publishing Company, 1989, 390.

79 Kenneth C. Martis, *The Historical Atlas of the Political Parties in the United States Congress, 1789–1989.* Macmillan Publishing Company, 1989, 109.

80 Joel H. Silbey, "After 'The First Northern Victory': The Republican Party Comes to Congress, 1855–1856." *The Journal of Interdisciplinary History* 20, no. 1, Summer 1989, 2. "Perhaps because of the large number of factions," Temple R. Hollcroft concurs, "*The Congressional Globe* did not follow its usual practice of indicating party affiliation in printing the list of members of the thirty-fourth Congress." Temple R. Hollcroft, "A Congressman's Letters on the Speaker Election in the Thirty-Fourth Congress." *The Mississippi Valley Historical Review* 43, no. 3, December 1956, 444.

81 "During the first session of the thirty-fourth Congress," Ohio's John Sherman, then serving his first term in the House recalled, "the opponents of slavery were without a party name or organization." Joel H. Silbey, "After 'The First Northern Victory': The Republican Party Comes to Congress, 1855–1856." *The Journal of Interdisciplinary History* 20, no. 1, Summer 1989, 4.

always had a single, clear party with enough seats to form a clean majority in each chamber. 1855 is the exception to this remarkable history of single, clear House and Senate majorities in Congress from 1789 to today.

Quarrels in this confusing scrum of lawmakers began almost immediately when the thirty-fourth Congress convened its first session. Mostly mundane matters – designation of the House members by party name in *The Congressional Record*, the dispensation of a House printer – instead became issues of dispute. Larger, more substantive matters – the selection of the House Speaker, major committee assignments in the chamber – took weeks to resolve. Galleries in the House were packed with visitors on most days to watch the beldam on the House floor below.[82] Nine weeks after it convened its first session, the House finally selected Rep. Nathaniel Banks of Massachusetts as the Speaker. He was selected on the one-hundred and thirty-third ballot on Tuesday, February 5, 1856 by just a three-vote margin, after no fewer than 17 different House members had thrown their hat in the ring for the job. "The final charge was now made, amid breathless anxiety and the most intense excitement," *The New York Daily Times* told its readers a day later on Wednesday, February 6, 1856. "The one-hundred and thirty-third ballot was now taken, the one which must decide the contest," *The New York Daily Times* said of the last ballot that Thursday electing Banks as Speaker.[83] The selection that Thursday of the Speaker marked the longest and most contentious such election ever in the history of the House, and it marked the last time in history that the Congress would not have a clear, single-party majority of Democrats or Republicans in the House or Senate chambers.

The thirty-fourth Congress seated in 1855 was a session like no other whose House majority was every bit as makeshift, messy, and muddled as America itself on the eve of the Civil War. As the floor debates and parliamentary fisticuffs that preoccupied so much of the thirty-fourth Congress brought little in the way of compromise, so too, outside of the Capitol's House and Senate chambers in the streets and in the statehouses in cities and towns across the country, millions of Americans saw it as a time not of compromise but of contention. America's conscience awakened with the stories of the escape and capture of fugitive slaves and the repulsion of so many Americans at the South's unapologetic defense of slavery, mustering at long last the stirrings of the second of the country's largest and most enduring political parties.

---

82 James G. Hollandsworth, Jr., *Pretense of Glory: The Life of General Nathaniel P. Banks*. Louisiana State University Press, 1998, 26.
83 "The Election of Mr. Banks to the Speakership, Exciting Scenes in the House." *The New York Daily Times* Wednesday, February 6, 1856, 2.

Chapter 3 The Emergence of the Republican Party and the Late Nineteenth Century Democratic and Republican Parties, 1854–1893

"We went in Whigs, Free Soilers, and Democrats. We came out Republicans," Alan E. Bovay said, looking back on the Wisconsin winter of 1854 when he and his neighbors made history in the small schoolhouse in their town of Ripon. The southeast Wisconsin town to this day is long remembered as a claimant for the location of the first local meeting of the Republican Party. Abolitionist Whigs, anti-slavery Democrats, and former Free Soilers met on Monday evening, March 20, 1854 in their town's schoolhouse to discuss the issues of the day, and in so doing, they made history as they walked out into the cold of the Winter night, marking the beginning of one of the most important chapters in America's history and founding one of country's oldest and most enduring political parties.

When Alan E. Bovay's neighbors gathered in their town's schoolhouse that March evening, they saw themselves as facing a fight against an evil of enslavement familiar to generations of Americans. Theirs was the fight of conscience against the extension of the South's slavery both into the territories to the west and in the capture and arrest of fugitive slaves in places like Wisconsin and elsewhere. What remnants of the Whigs, Free Soilers, and others were left in Ripon after 1852's election stirred against slavery's encroachment into their state in the arrest and return of fugitive slaves. The meeting in Ripon's schoolhouse that March evening in 1854 also took place just days after Illinois' Democratic Senator Stephen A. Douglas and Democrats in the Senate had made their latest stride in the extension of slavery in the territories to the west of Wisconsin.

Senator Douglas' bill passed in the Senate on Saturday, March 4, 1854 opening Nebraska and other western territories to slavery if the territories voted for it, what Michigan's Democratic Senator Lewis Cass and others at the time celebrated as squatter sovereignty.[84] A week after Douglas' bill passed in the Senate, a large crowd of Milwaukeans forced their way into a municipal jail to release Joshua Glover, an escaped slave being held while awaiting his return to his owner in Mis-

---

[84] "At five o'clock, the final vote was taken, and the bill passed – by Yeas, 37, Nays, 14," *The New York Daily Times* reported. "Mr. Cass [said] 'I congratulate the Senate on the triumph of squatter sovereignty.'" "Final Passage of the Nebraska Bill in the Senate." *The New York Daily Times* Monday, March 6, 1854, 5.

https://doi.org/10.1515/9783111340029-004

souri.[85] Glover's rescue on the evening of Saturday, March 11, 1854 by the crowd of anti-slavery Milwaukeeans came at a time when the flight of escaped slaves took on greater importance in the Great Lakes and Upper Midwest in places like Milwaukee and in towns like Ripon. Escaped slaves like Glover facing their flight to freedom through the Midwest where they hid in basements by day and swam across rivers by night touched the lives of Americans in towns like Ripon, and it touched off the meetings that began the building of the Republican Party.

Monday, March 20, 1854's meeting in the schoolhouse in Ripon, a building today on the National Register of Historic Places, is remembered as one of the first and most famous of a series of meetings in the spring and summer of 1854 along with other small towns like Crawfordsville, Iowa and Exeter, New Hampshire, also claimants to the history of these early local meetings of anti-slavery Democrats, abolitionist Whigs, and others. These meetings were watched closely by many, not least of which were newspaper editors like *The New York Tribune*'s Horace Greeley, *The Detroit Tribune*'s Joseph Warren, and others who'd seen the Whigs disappear with no new national party yet to take its place against the Democrats.

"In view of the necessity of battling for the first principles of republican government, and against the schemes of aristocracy the most revolting and oppressive with which the earth was ever cursed, or man debased, we will cooperate and be known as REPUBLICANS until the contest be terminated," Thursday, July 6, 1854's convention of more than 4,000 delegates in Jackson, Michigan declared in the first statewide convention of the Republican Party. *The Detroit Tribune*'s editor Joseph Warren publicized the convention weeks beforehand in his editorials and reporting. Thousands of anti-slavery Whigs, Free Soilers, and others following *The Detroit Tribune*'s calls arrived in the Michigan town in such large numbers that the meeting's initial location in Jackson's Bronson Hall, a building whose auditorium only seated some 600 persons, had to be moved outside to a nearby grove of oak trees then on the outskirts of the town where a stage was built for the convention's speakers to address the crowd. Today, Jackson remembers this location with a small park and several historical markers telling the story of 1854's convention.

"HERE UNDER THE OAKS, JULY 6, 1854, WAS BORN THE REPUBLICAN PARTY, DESTINED IN THE THROES OF CIVIL STRIFE TO ABOLISH SLAVERY, VINDICATE DEMOCRACY, AND PERPETUATE THE UNION," reads the oldest of these historical markers in Jackson, affixed to a large boulder near the corner of Second St. and Franklin St. that has been one of the most iconic and important locations in the

---

85 "A Fugitive Slave in Milwaukee, Excitement of the Citizens, the Jail Broken, the Fugitive Rescued, and the Military Ordered Out." *The New York Daily Times* Friday, March 17, 1854, 3.

history of the Republican Party. 1854's convention in Jackson was the first of a series of state conventions across the country that marked the formation of the Republican Party that Summer.

Wisconsin's state convention met on Thursday, July 13, 1854 at the state capital in Madison just a week after the convention in Jackson. Wisconsin's convention welcomed "all men opposed to the repeal of the Missouri Compromise and the extension of the Slave Power." Well over 3,000 people that Thursday assembled in Madison under the trees on the lawn surrounding the capitol for what its organizers called a People's Convention. "We met in the capitol park," Edwin Hurlbut, an Oconomowoc attorney and leader at the Madison convention later recalled of 1854's convention. "The steps of the old capitol [were] the rostrum," Hurlbut recalled. The crowd outside the Wisconsin capitol that Thursday selected a convention chairman, secretary, and members of a committee on resolutions. Delegates prepared the selection of a ticket of candidates for 1854's midterm, and approved the Republican name for the new Wisconsin party.[86] "We accept the issue forced upon us by the slave power, and, in defense of freedom, will cooperate and be known as Republicans," delegates declared in the shade of the trees of the Wisconsin capitol that Thursday. "The name caught the crowd, cheer upon cheer swept over the multitude, and the new organization was, by a unanimous vote, denominated the Republican Party," Hurlbut told Oconomowoc's *The Wisconsin Free Press* some years later.

Thursday, July 20, 1854's Worcester, Massachusetts convention was the next statewide gathering of the Republicans that summer.[87] "This convention invites

---

86 Once resolutions criticizing the repeal of the Missouri compromise and the fugitive slave bill were passed by the convention, Edwin Hurlbut recalled some years later his own part in the convention's adoption of the Republican name. "'Mr. Chairman,' I said, addressing that officer, 'I recall in my early manhood as I came across its threshold filled with hopes of possible achievement, the party of liberality, the party of the people was known as the Republican Democratic party. That was the party of Andrew Jackson. The party of Jefferson was known as the Republican Party.'" "'Let us, sir,'" Hurlbut recalled himself saying on the grounds of the old Wisconsin capitol, "'christen this child of promise after the party of Thomas Jefferson, that sterling representative of true Americanism.'"

87 A remarkable account of the mood of the day by one of the presiding officers at Worcester's July 20, 1854 convention, written by Stephen M. Allen on the twenty-fifth anniversary of that convention, tells of the moment bringing so many delegates to the convention: "It was a large meeting, spontaneous in fervor and spirit, representing citizens of all former political parties, and though coincident with, was in its origin independent of, similar outbursts of popular feeling in many other northern states. But one sentiment seemed to pervade all these gatherings at the North. As of one mind mysteriously moved, the great current set energetically in one direction. A tidal wave of popular will, seemingly inspired by Deity itself, was felt approaching, and the foundation of old political parties were giving away, and even the Union itself was felt to be in danger. Never

the Republicans of every town and city in the Commonwealth to send delegates to the number of three times their representatives in the [state legislature] to be held on Thursday, August 10, for the purpose of nominating candidates for state officers and forming a platform of state policy," it declared.[88] A crowd numbering some 600 met in the morning in Worcester's City Hall. By midday that Thursday, the arrival of a train carrying several hundred more attendees filled the City Hall to capacity, so it was agreed to recess temporarily until the early afternoon and then reconvene outside on the lawn of the Worcester town square, yet another meeting outdoors on the grass and under the trees like the Jackson and Madison conventions.

Wednesday, August 16, 1854's New York convention is one of the most important state conventions that summer, as a convention that included some of New York City's most influential newspaper editors. More than 500 delegates, representing 56 of the state's 59 counties, assembled in Saratoga Springs "for the purpose of expressing their views in relation to the growing aggressions and assumptions of the slave power."[89] "The spacious hall is full of the most sturdy and intellectual looking body of men ever convened in this State in a delegate convention," *The Albany Journal* reported that Wednesday.[90] *The New York Tribune*'s Horace Greeley, *The New York Daily Times*' Henry Raymond, and *The New York Evening Post*'s William Cullen Bryant all attended the Saratoga Springs convention.

Jackson. Madison. Worcester. Saratoga Springs. These conventions in July and August 1854 were followed by later meetings in other states to build the new Republicans Party. Michigan, Wisconsin, Massachusetts, and New York Republicans all adopted the Republican name at their 1854 conventions, this at a time when

---

but once before in the history of the country had such deep, determined feeling pervaded the masses, or the foundations of our civil government seemed so insecure. British injustice and arrogance being oppressive, and political crime against the manhood of our fathers had indeed once generated just such a spirit in the minds and hearts of American subjects, which proved an unquenchable fire, burning through the yokes of civil bondage and servitude, and melting and tearing off the political shackles which, once loosed, proclaimed and maintained the Republic. One dark spot only remained to cloud the social horizon of the best government the world ever knew, a legacy of sin, a stone not rejected by the builders, though cursed of God, abhorred by angels, and despised by men. This cloud of social and political wrong, after three quarters of a century, through the agencies of human selfishness, was fast overshadowing the whole land." Stephen M. Allen, *Origin and Early Progress of the Republican Party in the United States, Together with the History of its Formation in Massachusetts*. Getchell Brothers, 1879, 7–8.

88 Francis Curtis, *The Republican Party: A History of its 50 Years' Existence and a Record of its Measures and Leaders, 1854–1904, Volume I*. G.P. Putnam's Sons, 1904, 195–196.

89 William Barnes, *The Origin and Early History of the Republican Party*. J.B. Lyon Company Printers, 1906, 21–22.

90 William Barnes, *The Origin and Early History of the Republican Party*. J.B. Lyon Company Printers, 1906, 22.

some attending those conventions urged them to adopt names like the Freeman's Party, the Liberty and Union Party, or the Free Democrats. Delegates at some of these conventions had even considered calling themselves Democratic Republicans, a name that for some of those in attendance had a resonance in the history of the party of their fathers, the party of Jefferson, Madison, and Monroe. It was, finally, simply, a familiar name that was adopted, one that was a part of a history that had been used by Andrew Jackson's supporters before they called themselves Democrats as well as by Jackson's opponents in 1832's election.

Mid-nineteenth century America on the eve of the Civil War is a time when the confluence of changes in technology and transportation changed every aspect of America's presidential elections, and placed the Democrats and Republicans in the center of one of the most consequential moments in the history of the United States. Improvements in transportation offered the opportunity for Democrats and Republicans to travel to their national conventions, to circulate the latest news of their presidential candidates and their platforms during presidential elections by telegraph and steam-driven newspaper printing presses, and even opened the possibilities for candidates to break with their long-held custom of staying on the front porches of their homes and speaking to visiting crowds. Improvements in travel instead allowed large numbers of Democrats and Republicans to make cross-country trips to visit the towns of their nominees and to assemble in great gatherings by the many thousands to parade in front of the homes of presidential candidates for both the Democrats and the Republicans, and eventually led the candidates for President to leave their homes and travel across the country to meet voters.

Nominating conventions of both the Democrats and Republicans in the mid-nineteenth century grew to grand affairs, usually lasting at least a week or sometimes longer. Governors, Representatives, Senators, and other powerbrokers held sway in the hallways and hotel rooms, while the conventions haggled over their platforms, selected their nominees, and set out their strategies for victory. For the Democrats and Republicans, national nominating conventions in the mid-nineteenth century were a gauntlet navigated only by those candidates for President who'd carefully cultivated the support of a political party's insiders and established power-brokers. Democratic and Republican nominees for President in the mid- and late nineteenth century did not attend the nominating conventions in person, and by custom did no actual campaigning in person once selected by their national conventions, leaving this up to their vast, army-like national parties for the Democrats and Republicans after the Civil War.

America's mid- and late nineteenth century elections filled with familiar stories of the bribery, intimidation, and harassment of voters casting their ballots. Ballots still were printed by the Democrats and Republicans until the end of the nineteenth century. Votes were sometimes cast in glass-sided ballot-boxes under the watchful eye of local officials, but such measures did little to tamp down or temper fraud when some of these same local officials manipulated the counting of ballots to favor their own party.[91] Poll taxes, Constitution or literacy tests, and other manipulations trimmed the rolls of otherwise eligible voters, be it African Americans newly-enfranchised under the Fifteenth Amendment or newly arrived immigrants in northern cities who faced the humiliation of so-called reading tests to disqualify them. Whites-only state primaries and disenfranchisement bills enacted by southern legislatures effectively marked the end of any pretense that such measures were intended to ensure the education and qualification of all voters – as the names of such measures, be they literacy bills or whites only primaries, expressed their exclusionary intent in the disqualification of specific groups of voters, be they illiterate or unable to afford poll taxes or freed slaves and their descendants.

June 1856's Democratic National Convention made history as the third nominating convention to strike a sitting President from a party's national ticket. Meeting in Cincinnati in June 1856, the Democratic National Convention for the first time struck a sitting Democratic President, President Franklin Pierce, from its national ticket. Democrats at their convention selected Pennsylvania's James Buchanan as the replacement for Pierce.[92] 1856's election marked the first national ticket for the Republicans, led by John C. Fremont of California and William L. Dayton of New Jersey. Fremont fell short in facing the ticket of James Buchanan and his Vice-Presidential running mate, John C. Breckinridge of Kentucky, a disappointment for the newly-created Republicans. Still, in that same election, 1856 saw Republicans carry a number of House seats in districts stretching across the Upper Midwest from Iowa's first and second districts into northern Illinois and Indiana, sweeping down into southeastern Ohio and Pennsylvania, and then continuing up into the Northeast with nearly all of New York's House seats carried by Republicans, along with sweeping the entire House delegations in Maine, Massachusetts, New Hampshire, and Vermont.[93] In the Senate, the Republicans carried an impressive 20 Senate seats in their first showing in 1856 to the 41 held by the Democrats in that chamber.

---

91 Peter H. Argersinger, "New Perspectives on Election Fraud in the Gilded Age." *Political Science Quarterly* 100, no. 4, Winter 1985, pp. 669 – 687.
92 "Democratic National Convention, Fifth and Last Day, the Nominations Made, James Buchanan for President, John C. Breckinridge for Vice President, Exciting Scenes, Speech of Mr. Breckinridge, How the Nominations are Received." *The New York Daily Times* Saturday, June 7, 1856, 1.
93 Kenneth C. Martis, *The Historical Atlas of the Political Parties in the United States Congress, 1789 – 1989.* Macmillan Publishing Company, 1989, 111.

Having taken a one-term pledge when accepting his nomination by the Democratic National Convention, President James Buchanan's four-year term marked effectively a placeholder for a wide-open national contest in 1860. 1860 offered a promising opening for the Republicans after they'd fallen short in 1856.[94] Little did the Republicans imagine at the time that their nominee for 1860's national ticket, a recently-defeated Illinois Republican Senate candidate who'd lost his bid just two years earlier to Senator Stephen Douglas, would face a Democratic Party as divided as any to date in its history.

Never in the history of the Democrats, Whigs, and Republicans had any national convention ever assembled and then adjourned without the selection of a Presidential and Vice Presidential ticket. That changed in April 1860. That year's Democratic National Convention in Charleston, South Carolina is an extraordinary chapter in the history of political parties in the United States, as the first and only nominating convention that recessed after days of deadlock among Democratic delegations with no presidential ticket for the Fall's contest. Failure to select a national ticket happened only this one time in the history of political parties in the United States, and it happened in the exact same meeting hall where the Constitution and the union itself would face its ultimate test only a month after 1860's election.

When Democrats traveling from across the country gathered in Charleston in April 1860, the coastal Carolina city seethed as a seedbed of secessionist sentiment. A coterie of secession-minded publishers and officeholders in Charleston were determined to scuttle the nomination of Senator Douglas at all costs, even in the absence of any other Democratic candidate able to muster the two-thirds of convention delegates. Robert Barnwell Rhett, Jr.'s *The Charleston Mercury* primed the Douglas delegates with editorials railing against the Illinois Democrat in his paper.

Charleston's Institute Hall was the setting for what became one of the most extraordinary moments in the history of political parties in the United States, and might just as easily have been the moment where the Democratic Party disappeared forever. Arriving Democratic delegates to Charleston made their way to the city's Institute Hall. What they found there exceeded their fears of the formidable challenges facing Douglas' supporters. For months, Douglas' supporters had sought a location anywhere other than Charleston. "Charleston is the last place on God's Earth where a national convention should have been held," Thomas Dyer, one of Illinois' delegates supporting Douglas, said.

---

94 *Official Proceedings of the National Democratic Convention, Held in Cincinnati, June 2 – 6, 1856.* Enquirer Company Steam Printing Establishment, 1856, 77.

After several days of preliminary proceedings in Institute Hall, the hour finally arrived for state delegations to start their difficult path to reaching the two-thirds of delegates needed for the selection of a ticket for November. Suddenly, one after another, delegates from eight states including South Carolina's host delegation announced their departure and walked out of Institute Hall, this before even the first ballot was cast for the nomination of the November ticket.[95] When the eight Democratic delegations left Institute Hall on Monday, April 30, 1860, it became obvious to the delegates still in the hall that the convention now faced the nearly impossible task of nominating a winning national ticket by two-thirds of the remaining delegates.[96] Douglass carried a majority of delegates in each vote, but ballot after ballot ended up with Douglas unable to reach the required two-thirds of delegates. With some 57 ballots cast in Institute Hall, Democrats finally did something no other nominating convention has ever done: announce its adjournment with no ticket for President and Vice President.

In almost every respect, Chicago's selection as the location for 1860's Republican National Convention was as fortuitous for the Republicans as Charleston's selection was fatal for the Democrats. Republicans who'd selected Chicago at their national meeting in December 1859 hoped the selection of the city would help the Republican ticket carry Illinois and several other key states in the Midwest. Careful maneuvering by home-state supporters of Abraham Lincoln, including *The Chicago Daily Press and Tribune*'s editor Joseph Medill, finally gained enough backing for the Springfield attorney and former Whig Representative that, on the third ballot after it became clear that New York's William Seward lacked sufficient support, Lincoln emerged with the Republican nomination in Chicago.

"We've found an honest man," Republicans celebrated in Chicago on Friday, May 18, 1860, exuberant in their party's nomination of a Fall ticket while the Democrats faced the fallout from Charleston.[97] When all was said and done, Lincoln and his running-mate Sen. Hannibal Hamlin faced two Democratic tickets that fall – one, a Democratic ticket of then-Vice President John C. Breckinridge selected in Baltimore by what *The New York Daily Times* and other papers called the Seceders' convention, and the other, Senator Douglas, who won his spot on a national

---

95 "The delegations of eight Cotton States had formally 'absolved themselves' from all connection with the National Democratic Party." George Fort Milton, *The Eve of Conflict: Stephen A. Douglas and the Needless War.* Houghton Mifflin Company, 1934, 450.

96 "Secession of the Southern Delegations, Davis and Everett Proposed by the Bolters." *The New York Times* Tuesday, May 1, 1860, 1.

97 "Republican Nominations, for President of the United States, Abraham Lincoln of Illinois, for Vice President, Hannibal Hamlin of Maine, for the Great Presidential Campaign." *The Chicago Press and Tribune* Saturday, May 19, 1860, 1.

ticket when a second Democratic convention of what became known as National Democrats convened in June 1860.

That fall, Republican nominee Abraham Lincoln, Democrat Stephen Douglas, then-Vice President John Breckinridge, and Tennessee's John Bell as the candidate of the short-lived Constitutional Union ticket all held to the long custom of staying at their homes and saying little besides limited remarks to those party supporters traveling to visit with them at their homes. Springfield saw some of the largest crowds ever to visit the hometown of a presidential candidate as large parades and rallies were held in the streets of the Illinois capital, parading in front of Lincoln's home on the corner of Eighth Street and Jackson Street. Today, the U.S. National Park Service's Lincoln Home National Historic Site with its closed-off streets in the neighborhood allows visitors to walk the tree-shaded neighborhood and imagine the hundreds of horse-drawn wagons, many emblazoned with Abraham Lincoln's name, that would have been steered by their drivers past the front-steps of the Republican nominee's home. Wide Awakes, Bell Ringers, and Little Giants took to the streets in cities and towns across the United States in 1860 in great processions, sometimes clad in military-style uniforms and parading with torches late into the evenings.

Tuesday, November 6, 1860's election of President-elect Abraham Lincoln with some 180 Electoral votes and 18 out of 33 states was an extraordinary moment. Telegraphs whirred throughout the night while printing presses clattered away at many of the nation's newspapers rushing to deliver overnight reports of the election returns.[98] From the telegraph offices near his home in Springfield, Abraham Lincoln stayed up late pouring over state-by-state returns and then went to bed in the early morning hours of that Wednesday, confident in his election as the first Republican President, as well as holding the Republican House majority and securing a Senate majority for the Republicans for the first time.

"The tea has been thrown overboard, the revolution of 1860 has been initiated," *The Charleston Mercury* told its readers the day after Lincoln's election. "Yesterday, November seventh, will long be a memorable day in Charleston," *The Charleston Mercury* said, as the news of Lincoln's election spread on the streets of the coastal city. "The greatest excitement prevailed, and the news spread with lightning rapidity over the city," *The Charleston Mercury* told its readers of the "long and continued cheering for a Southern Confederacy" that could be heard up

---

98 "Only in New Jersey, California, and Oregon," William E. Gienapp tells us, "did Lincoln's margin of victory result from the division of the opposition vote, and these states provided him with only 11 Electoral votes." William E. Gienapp, "Who Voted for Lincoln?" In John L. Thomas (ed.) *Abraham Lincoln and the American Political Tradition.* The University of Massachusetts Press, 1986, 62.

and down the sidewalks in front of *The Mercury*'s offices.[99] Celebrations of the news of their defeat by Lincoln and cheers for their certainty of secession still echoed through the streets of Charleston when Thursday, December 20, 1860's vote in Institute Hall was taken for South Carolina's Ordinance of Secession, barely a month after the election. Today, the city's historical marker at the old location of Institute Hall on Market Street, a building that was lost to fire in December 1861, tells this story. One side of the marker ("INSTITUTE HALL") tells visitors of the deadlock and adjournment of April 1860's Democratic National Convention. The other side of the marker ("THE UNION IS DISSOLVED!") tells the story of the secession convention.[100] Weeks later and just blocks away from Institute Hall, the shelling of Fort Sumter commenced at 4:30 A.M. on Friday morning, April 12, 1861, beginning a war for the survival of the Union that ends in the Virginia countryside almost exactly 4 years from the date it began.

Institute Hall and Fort Sumter are a world away from the wooded hillsides at the feet of the Blue Ridge Mountains surrounding the two-story red-brick courthouse of Appomattox County, Virginia, where the war came to an end in surrender's stillness at 4:00 P.M. on Sunday, April 9, 1865. The "revolution of 1860," as *The Charleston Mercury* had said in November 1860, was finished, but another revolution far more worthy of the losses and sacrifices of wartime was just starting as the Thirteenth Amendment to the Constitution had already been sent to the states for ratification by the time of the Appomattox surrender. Some 20 states had already ratified the Thirteenth Amendment abolishing slavery by the day of the war's end on Sunday, April 9, 1865.

In the painful months after President Abraham Lincoln's assassination at Ford's Theater in Washington and his death in a home across the street on Saturday, April 15, 1865, Democrats and Republicans found themselves in the difficult days that followed the first assassination of a President. From almost the very moment of the death of President Lincoln, the battles between the Democrats and the Republicans almost immediately plunged the country into political conflict, con-

---

99 "The News of Lincoln's Election." *The Charleston Mercury* Thursday, November 8, 1860, 1. *The Charleston Mercury* reported that Wednesday on the "great excitement" on the streets of Charleston as "a large number of enthusiastic gentlemen, having congregated, anxiously [awaited] the result of the presidential election." "Upon the announcement of [Lincoln's election] at the *Mercury* office, which appeared to be the headquarters for information," *The Charleston Mercury* reported on Wednesday, "the crowd gave expression to their feelings by long and continued cheering for a Southern Confederacy." "The Presidential Election." *The Charleston Mercury* Wednesday, November 7, 1860, 2.

100 "The Twentieth Day of December, in the Year of Our Lord, 1860." *The Charleston Mercury* Friday, December 21, 1860, 1.

frontation, and controversy unlike anything ever seen in the country's history. Taking a page out of the negative partisanship that drives elections in the early decades of the twenty-first century, Democrats and Republicans pitched their struggles for votes in the language of war. Both Democrats and Republicans "waved the bloody shirt" with more stalwart loyalists of both the Democrats and Republicans urging their supporters to "vote as you shot." Democrats and Republicans made every appeal they could to every memory, however painful these might be, to turn out voters in the years after the Civil War. Democrats and Republicans thought nothing of using whatever means at their disposal to win their races in what has been christened by historian Mark Wahlgren Summers as the era of good stealings, whether in the form of harassment and intimidation of voters to steal elections or in the buying and selling of votes.[101]

What is most remarkable about the years after the Civil War is just how closely contested so many races were in so many parts of the country, and the survival of the Democratic Party to make elections so closely competitive with the Republicans so soon after the war's end. Close elections between the Democrats and Republicans opened the door to all manner of election fraud, as the Democrats and Republicans sought whatever advantages they could in the handful of states that decided presidential elections after the Civil War. The late nineteenth century's closeness in elections drove all manner of voter fraud and this, in turn, prompted a generation of reform-minded elected officials to eventually address those election irregularities through a new era of reforms.

More than ever, almost every presidential election in the late nineteenth century turned on a handful of states, usually half a dozen or so states including Indiana, New York, Ohio, and Pennsylvania. Handbills, pamphlets, and printed materials of all kinds flooded these states, as did the money that bought and sold votes in what in some precincts was effectively open-bidding between Democrats and Republicans for voters. In the later part of the nineteenth century, voters sometimes crossed state lines to cast votes in neighboring states. They cast ballots in different precincts on the same day, and sometimes impersonated or posed as deceased persons to cast additional ballots.[102] "To prove the age corrupt would

---

101 Mark Wahlgren Summers, *The Era of Good Stealings*. Oxford University Press, 1993.

102 "Vote buying added to parties' costs," Mark Wahlgren Summers reminds us, "and so did thwarting the rascals, the repeaters and 'colonizers' from other states, the armies of strangers sheltered in city flophouses that trooped to the polls to vote under the names of the dead, absent, and inconveniently late electors still registered on the books, when any real registration procedures existed at all." Mark Wahlgren Summers, "'To Make the Wheels Revolve We Must Have Grease': Barrel Politics in the Gilded Age." *The Journal of Policy History* 14, no. 1, January 2002, 56 – 57.

waste paper and ink," historian Mark Wahlgren Summers tells us.[103] While the closeness of elections nationally and the fraud accompanying it brought elections in the United States to a new low, strides were made by the end of the nineteenth-century to establish newer procedures for more well-organized recordkeeping in the lists and verification of names of voters and the use of state-printed, standardized ballots.

President Abraham Lincoln's death in the early morning hours of Saturday, April 15, 1865, left the nation in mourning, but few Democratic or Republican powerbrokers had the time to mourn alongside the nation as the nation's capital prepared for what many knew was the stormy succession of President Andrew Johnson. The late President Lincoln had selected Johnson in the spirit of forming a unity ticket to appeal to a larger segment of the country in a time of disunion and war, yet it was Lincoln's death and the succession of Johnson that precipitated one of the most contentious moments in the history of the country.

Vetoing 21 bills enacted by a Republican-led Congress, President Andrew Johnson has the distinction of having the largest number of vetoes overridden ever for any President in history, 15 of his 21 vetoes overridden by the House and senate. President Johnson's veto of the Tenure of Office Act and its override by the House and Senate in March 1867 proved to be a breaking point in his relationship with the Republican Congress, as eight of the eleven articles of impeachment voted by the House against Johnson on Monday, February 24, 1868 directly addressed Johnson's veto of the Tenure of Office Act.[104] Weeks later, on Saturday, May 16, 1868, the Senate fell just one vote shy of the two-thirds needed to remove Johnson from office, the closest that any impeached President has ever come to removal by a vote of the Senate.

With the election of President Ulysses Grant in 1868 and his reelection in 1872, Tuesday, November 7, 1876's election is remembered as the centennial election where the competitiveness and the closeness of the campaign contest between New York's Democratic Governor Samuel Tilden against Republican Ohio Governor Rutherford Hayes upended the country's presidential elections. 1876's presidential election split the country in half, sparked fears of violence as the outcome hung in the balance for months, and brought still more attention to election fraud and corruption in many parts of the country, especially the handful of closely-competitive states that determined the outcome of the country's presidential elections.

---

103 Mark Wahlgren Summers, *The Era of Good Stealings*. Oxford University Press, 1993, viii.

104 "Debate in the House on the Impeachment Resolution, the Resolution Adopted by a Vote of 126 to 47, the President to be Arraigned for Trial Immediately, Gen. Thomas Makes Another Unsuccessful Attempt to Oust Secretary Stanton, Message of the President Defending His Action in Removing Mr. Stanton." *The New York Times* Tuesday, February 25, 1868, 1.

Republicans rallied against the "blood-stained hands of the Rebels" and called Democrats the party of treason. Democrats spoke of charges of corruption in the Grant White House to make inroads against the Republicans. Tilden's popular vote majority nationally was thought to have bested his opponent by approximately one-quarter million more votes than Hayes, but the immediate and pressing focus centered not on the popular votes nationally but rather on the disputed outcomes of election tallies in the three states that together would determine the election's outcome: Florida, South Carolina, and Louisiana.

Wednesday, November 7, 1876 dawned with the chaotic and confusing counts from three of the country's most closely divided states. Tilden had won some 184 Electoral votes, just one shy of the 185 needed to win the White House. However, disputed returns in Florida, Louisiana, and South Carolina now plunged the nation into confusion. In Louisiana, Democrats claimed the Tilden ticket carried that state by some 20,000, votes while Republicans insisted Hays bested Tilden by some 4,000 ballots.[105] Florida and South Carolina's narrow margins drove the confusion still further. Cries of a stolen election by Governor Tilden's supporters grew louder and angrier as the controversy dragged on.

"There was talk among the more headlong and reckless partisans of each side of taking the law into their own hands," Princeton University's Woodrow Wilson wrote in his 1902 *A History of the American People.* "There were signs almost of civil war in the air for a few troubled weeks that anxious Autumn," Wilson later said.[106] Instead, cooler heads carried the day, but not before bringing the United States to the brink of violence and coming at the cost of the abandonment of the promise of the Fourteenth Amendment, the Fifteenth Amendment, and the end of enforcement of March 1875's Civil Rights Act.

With weeks of rumors swirling in Washington and across the country as the House and Senate faced the task of sorting out the mess of two sets of Electoral certifications arriving in Washington from Florida, Louisiana, and South Carolina. After much back-and-forth, the Democratic-led House and Republican-led Senate agreed to empanel a 15-member commission to sort out the double returns from Florida, Louisiana, and South Carolina. Meeting in the Supreme Court's chambers in the Capitol with five House members, five Senate members, and five Supreme Court Justices, the fifteen-member commission spent the next several weeks inves-

---

105 Alexander Clarence Flick, *Samuel Jones Tilden: A Study in Political Sagacity.* Kennikat Press, 1939, 326.
106 Woodrow Wilson, *A History of the American People, Illustrated with Portraits, Maps, Plans, Facsimiles, Rare Prints, Contemporary Views, Etc. in Five Volumes, Volume V.* Harper and Brothers Publishers, 1902, 110.

tigating the ballot disputes, all while rumors circulated of behind-the-scenes, closed-door negotiations in Washington to resolve the election.

On Friday, February 9, 1877, the 15-member Election Commission finally announced its first certification in the disputed balloting: it awarded Florida's four Electoral votes to Republican Rutherford Hayes.[107] Exactly one week later, on Friday, February 16, 1877, the commission certified Louisiana's eight Electoral votes for Hayes.[108] Finishing its work, the commission on Tuesday, February 27, 1877, certified South Carolina's seven Electoral votes for the Republican ticket.[109] Each of these votes were a tally of eight to seven by the commission. The last meeting that Tuesday came the day after a closed-door meeting said to be held by Democrats and Republicans at Wormley's Hotel just a few blocks from the White House, reportedly to firm up days of back-room, behind-the-scenes deals struck by Democrats and Republicans.[110] Following several more days of debate in the House, the Democratic-led chamber finally declared Republican Rutherford Hayes President in the early-morning hours of Friday, March 2, 1877.

On Monday, March 5, 1877, President Rutherford B. Hayes took office with his pledge from his Saturday, July 8, 1876 letter accepting his nomination, to serve only one four-year term.[111] With Hayes' one-term pledge and with Tilden's decision not

---

107 "The Electoral Tribunal, Florida's Four Votes for Hayes and Wheeler, Decision of the Case by a Vote of Eight to Seven after Ten Hours in Secret Session, No Separate Vote on the Eligibility of Mr. Humphreys, the Reasons Given for the Decision, Character and Incidents of the Debate, the Florida Case Believed to Carry Louisiana, a Joint Meeting of Congress Today to Continue the Count." *The New York Times* Saturday, February 10, 1877, 1.

108 "Louisiana for Governor Hayes, Action of the Electoral Tribunal, Resolute Refusal to go Behind the Lawful Act of the State, Evidence Beyond the State Certification Excluded, a Proposition to Permit Further Argument Declined by Counsel on Both Sides, the Eight Votes of Louisiana Counted for Hayes and Wheeler by Eight to Seven, a New Democratic Project for Delay." *The New York Times* Saturday, February 17, 1877, 1.

109 "The Electoral Tribunal, South Carolina for Hayes, Democratic Lawyers and Commissioners Talking to Consume Time, no Arguments on the Republican Side Except by the Objector, Mr. Lawrence, the Democratic Commissioners Evidently Cognizant of the Action of the House, the Disposition to Talk Less Manifest after the Adjournment of the House." *The New York Times* Wednesday, February 28, 1877, 1.

110 Bill Severn, *Samuel J. Tilden and the Stolen Election.* Ives Washburn, Inc., 1968, 197.

111 "The New Administration, President Hayes Takes His Seat, a Grand Popular Demonstration, an Event Promising Peace and Prosperity to the County, Washington Aglow with Enthusiasm over the Result of a Bitter Contest, Farewell to the Old and Welcome to the New Administration, the White House Changes Tenants." *The New York Times* Tuesday, March 6, 1877, 1. In his official letter of acceptance of the Republican nomination on Saturday, July 8, 1876, from Columbus, then-Governor Hayes pledged, if elected, to serve just one four-year term in the White House. "The declaration of principles by the Cincinnati convention makes no announcement in favor of a single Presidential term," Hayes wrote in his letter. "I do not assume to add to that declaration,

Massachusetts became a model of laws adopted by some thirty-eight states in the years between 1888 and 1892.[121] "Rarely in the history of the United States has a reform movement spread so quickly and successfully," Jerrold G. Rusk tells us, and, one might add, rarely in the history of the United States had a former President, let alone a defeated former President, taken such a forceful and forthright stand on such a reform-minded issue.[122] Grover Cleveland hadn't spent 4 years talking about amending the Constitution to replace the Electoral College, but instead spoke in support of state printed, stand-alone ballots and similar election reforms.

Tuesday, November 8, 1892's election pitting Republican President Benjamin Harrison against Democratic President Grover Cleveland is a rematch from Tuesday, November 6, 1888's contest.[123] Harrison's 1892 loss is the fifth sitting President in the history of the United States to be defeated in running for reelection.[124] Democrat Cleveland carried 23 states for a total of 277 Electoral votes to President Har-

---

121 "[In December 1889, President Grover Cleveland] was asked to give an address to the Merchants' Association of Boston. Cleveland decided to take a strong stand on ballot reform…The effect of the speech was electric…as the Australian ballot law became the law in state after state, Cleveland's speech was revealed as the unintentional opening shot of his triumphant nomination…and return to office in 1892." L.E. Fredman, *The Australian Ballot: The Story of an American Reform.* Michigan State University Press, 1968, 56 – 57. President Cleveland's address to the banquet of the Merchants' Association of Boston on Thursday evening, December 12, 1889, included the President's gratitude and thanks to Massachusetts – "She [has] been first to adopt a thorough scheme of ballot reform and to prove in practice its value and the invalidity of the objections made against it. We thank Massachusetts tonight for all that she has done for these reforms" – and pledged to lead his home state of New York and other states "in the enforcement and an effective and honest measure of ballot reform." "Cleveland Was the Lion, The Central Figure at a Notable Banquet, He Addresses the Merchants' Association and is Received with Enthusiasm." *The New York Times* Friday, December 13, 1889, 1, 2.
122 Jerrold G. Rusk, "The Effect of the Australian Ballot Reform on Split Ticket Voting, 1876 – 1908." *The American Political Science Review* 64, no. 4, December 1970, 1221.
123 "The presidential election of 1892 offered an extraordinary contrast with the previous contest. There seemed to be more factual argument and fewer noisy processions, and the day itself was generally quiet and orderly. The same candidates were running, Benjamin Harrison and Grover Cleveland, two solid citizens, well-known and widely-respected…but the most obvious explanation of the change was the adoption in the interval of the Australian ballot in 38 states." L.E. Fredman, *The Australian Ballot: The Story of an American Reform.* Michigan State University Press, 1968,83.
124 "Cleveland! Democrats Have Scored an Overwhelming Victory, New York State Swings at Tammany's Bidding, Vote in the Upper Counties too Small to Overcome that Below, Indiana Returns Mixed but the Democrats are in the Lead, Later Returns are not Likely to Change the Situation, Slow Returns Caused by the Working of the New Ballot Laws, California Democratic by 7,000." *The Chicago Daily Tribune* Wednesday, November 9, 1892, 1.

rison's 145 Electoral votes in 16 states.[125] That November's election was a windfall for the Democrats: for the first time since before the Civil War, a Democratic President entered the White House with a Democratic-led House and a Democratic-led Senate. Democrats who'd almost imploded in Charleston and could have been finished in the aftermath of the Civil War instead survived and thrived by 1892's sweep of the national election. Republican confidence plummeted for the first time in at the end of the nineteenth century, yet little did either the Democrats or Republicans know just how much would be upended with the financial collapse that awaited President Cleveland on his return to the White House in the spring of 1893, and little did they know that the party of Jackson, Van Buren, Polk, and Pierce, seemingly stronger than ever with Cleveland's election and that of Congress, would be left in a shambles in a matter of months.

---

125 "Complete Popular Vote for Presidential Electors, Tuesday, November 8, 1892." *The New York Times* Tuesday, January 10, 1893, 3.

Chapter 4 The Era of Primaries and Change in the Early Twentieth Century Democratic and Republican Parties, 1896–1928

"We stand at Armageddon, and we battle for the Lord," the speaker thundered to the crowd of some 1,000 delegates and an even larger audience in attendance on Monday, August 5, 1912. A crowd estimated at some 8,000 by *The Chicago Daily Tribune* filled the old Chicago Coliseum on the near Southside. "We fight in honorable fashion for the good of mankind, fearless of the future, unheeding of our individual fates, with unflinching hearts and undimmed eyes," the speaker told his audience. The speaker paced back and forth on stage as he spoke to the delegates and his audience on the opening afternoon of their convention. Affixed to the front of the stage, someone had mounted the trophy head of a full-grown bull moose, the large antlers looming over the delegates crowded on the floor of the Coliseum below the stage. In the black-and-white photographs appearing that next morning in the country's newspapers, the mounted head of the large bull moose was in almost every picture, some featuring the speaker holding his arms aloft and gesturing with characteristic bravado to his audience. The delegates and their family and friends that Monday afternoon had traveled some distance from across the country as delegates to the National Progressive Convention. The speaker standing on the stage was President Theodore Roosevelt.

Weeks after he'd traveled by train from his home in New York's Oyster Bay to Chicago to attend the Republican National Convention, Roosevelt once again traveled by train back to Chicago in the first week in August to speak to the National Progressive Convention, the same coliseum that had hosted June's Republican National Convention that President Roosevelt had left in such disappointment weeks earlier. An enthusiastic Roosevelt now stood before the National Progressive Convention's cheering delegates whose even louder applause awaited him days later when he accepted the convention's nomination for President. Roosevelt's Progressive ticket was almost certain to divide Republican voters and almost as certain to deliver the White House to the Democrats for the first time since 1892's election.

Having spent a long and difficult year seeking the presidential nomination of his Republican Party, Roosevelt knew well as he stood on stage in the Coliseum addressing the Progressive convention of the history he'd made months earlier, when he took part in the first party-splitting primary challenge ever against a sitting President. Roosevelt had run against his old friend, President William Howard Taft, in the 13 newly-minted presidential primary elections. Oregon and Wisconsin had enacted some of the first such primaries in their states giving their citizens more say in the selection of candidates for state offices and the selection of Senators, eventually expanding to the selection of delegates for presidential nominees for the Democrats and Republicans. By 1912, the list of states with presidential primaries grew to include California, Nebraska, New Jersey, North Dakota, and other states. What Roosevelt had undertaken as he campaigned that Spring was a candidacy that would, at best, win him just a handful of state primaries and with these just a handful of delegates for the Republican convention to try to do what hadn't been done since June 1884, namely remove a sitting President, William Howard Taft, from the 1912 Republican ballot and replace him with Roosevelt.

Not since Friday, June 6, 1884, on the fourth ballot defeating President Chester A. Arthur at the Republican National Convention and removing him from 1884's national ticket, had a sitting President been struck from its fall ticket by a party convention. Now, with the backing of the tens of thousands of Republican primary voters who'd cast their votes for Roosevelt in the nine primary states that Roosevelt had won in his four exhausting months of crisscrossing the country, Roosevelt attempted the seemingly impossible task of replacing his old friend, President Taft. Roosevelt's primary bid had already made Taft do something no other sitting President had ever done before in the country's history, namely travel to a dozen or so states by train to make his case to his fellow Republicans why he, Taft, should stay on their national ticket that Fall. President Lyndon Johnson, President Gerald Ford, and others would do the same years later.

Now back in Chicago in August 1912, Roosevelt stood on stage in the Coliseum surrounded by thunderous applause and the cheers of delegates for the Progressive convention. Roosevelt by all appearances seemed confident in accepting his nomination by the delegates to run as its candidate on 1912's ballot.[126] All but assuring a split in the votes cast that November by millions of Republican voters torn between Taft and Roosevelt, Republicans in all parts of the United States watched in disbelief at the scene playing out on the Coliseum's stage in Chicago, a scene all too fitting for a twentieth century where the lessening of old loyalties and attachments to the nation's Democrats and Republicans promised to change politics and elevate individual presidential candidates in their appeal directly to voters in ways hardly imaginable just a few years earlier at the end of the nineteenth century.

Roosevelt's acceptance of the Progressive nomination with Vice-Presidential running mate Governor Hiram Johnson of California seemed well in keeping

---

126 "New Party Opens Convention Today as Colonel Comes, Roosevelt Will Confer with National Progressive Leaders before the Meeting, All Allowed to Talk, Platform Outlined which is Expected to Create New Era in Politics, Beveridge to Give Keynote." *The Chicago Daily Tribune* Monday, August 5, 1912, 1.

with the precedent-shattering changes in the lives of almost every American in the first decade of the twentieth century. From the automobiles that now crowded the streets of cities like Chicago and jostled for space with pedestrians and city trolleys to the black-and-white silent motion pictures entertaining audiences across the country to the electricity that now lit the night as bright as day in downtowns like Chicago and that stretched electric lines from wooden pole to wooden pole in the more distant towns of the United States, the lives of Americans were changing quickly, and so too was America's presidential campaigning.

In some respects, the excitement of Roosevelt's candidacy and its challenge in 1912's election for President Taft and Democrat Woodrow Wilson could understandably be seen by many at the time as the beginning of the end for the place of the Democrats and Republicans in the nation's political life. And yet, the Republicans and Democrats remained enduringly familiar and seemingly unchanging constants in American life, two extraordinary, seemingly unshakable institutions with long histories and settled traditions stretching back generations. Democrats and Republicans, as much as they differed, shared a history of resilience that allowed them to survive and to thrive in the face of almost every challenge. Democrats and Republicans together were almost like an unbreakable, unshakeable habit for America's voters. In a world of breathtaking change and split-second invention, Democrats and Republicans, these two, familiar choices on a ballot, were welcomed by voters eager to finish the bruising battles of Fall campaigns and put them behind them in November knowing the stewards of governance for the country over the next two years. America's restless, boundless energy for moving forward fit the familiar, simple choices of the Democrats and Republicans on the ballot. A Democrat or Republican would win the White House. Either the Democrats or the Republicans would win the Senate. Democrats or Republicans, one or the other, would win the House. The country could wake up first-thing Wednesday morning after an election knowing exactly who won what, and get back to business. The voters had spoken and now the country could get back to work. No sudden moves. No surprises. Democrats and Republicans – familiar, simple, uncomplicated.

In a twentieth century where change was the constant in almost every part of the lives of Americans, Democrats and Republicans were constants that withstood almost every change whether in the form of new political parties or the independent candidacies of individuals with the ability or the means to reach the voters directly, even, say, a popular former President's bid for the Presidency. Democrats and Republicans started the twentieth century with the challenge of the President Theodore Roosevelt and Progressive Party, and they ended the twentieth century as some of the most remarkably changing-yet-unchanged of all institutions in the history of the United States. Democrats and Republicans proved themselves extraordinarily enduring institutions capable of absorbing and adapting to almost every challenge and long outlasting the endless predictions of their impending disappearance or irrelevance.

At the end of the nineteenth century, Democrats and Republicans both accumulated decades of expertise in reaching voters in all parts of the country, in small towns and large cities, with every available means of taking their messages, platforms, and candidates to the country. Rallies, marches, speeches, parades, marching bands, sheet music, banners, buttons, pins, and endless trinkets of all kinds were commonplace. Anything and everything that the Democrats and Republicans had within their reach at the end of the nineteenth century was used to reach their supporters and to appeal to voters. Democrats and Republicans threw everything they had into campaigning in every part of the country, adopting every trick to take their messages to the people, whether it was shoring up the enthusiasm of their more loyal supporters or making the careful and considerate case for those undecided voters still on the fence in an election. Vast sums were spent by the Democrats and Republicans on everything from banners and newspapers to parades, marching bands, and anything else that entertained and enlivened campaigning in the nineteenth century. When the appeals to the voters through handbills, parades, and speeches were not enough, Democrats and Republicans were still well-accustomed in some parts of the country to the payment of money for those voters willing to sell their votes to the highest bidder.

At the end of the nineteenth century and still into the early twentieth century, national nominating conventions by long custom were still not attended in person by the nominees themselves, allowing their supporters to make their case on their behalf while the nominees waited for news at home of their nominations. Nominees for President still mostly remained on their front-porches during the fall campaign at the start of the twentieth century. However, Democratic and Republican nominees for President by the end of the first decade of the twentieth century began to look at traveling during their fall campaigns to reach voters in cities and towns across the United States, even if in-person attendance at the national conventions for presidential candidates was still another two or three decades away.

By the end of the nineteenth century, Democrats and Republicans both adapted to the state-by-state reforms of the day that started to change the way elections were held, including reforms at the state level that made the buying and selling votes more difficult for those who'd not given a second thought to buying, selling, and stealing votes just a few years earlier. The standardized ballots adopted by states beginning with Massachusetts in 1888, and growing to some 38 states by 1892, made it more difficult for voters to cast large numbers of artfully concealed and carefully folded paper-ballots tossed together into ballot boxes. Well-organized recordkeeping in the lists and verification of names of voters and the use of government-printed, standardized ballots by states at the end of the nineteenth century made it challenging to cast multiple ballots in different precincts on the same day, something that still continued in some places into the twentieth century, but now much more frowned upon in the twentieth century than it had been in the nineteenth.

Nationally, Democrats and Republicans kept up with these changes with ever more impressive professionally run operations and organizations at the turn-of-the-century. Early twentieth century innovations in commercial radio broadcasting at the end of the First World War and the push for the adoption of presidential primary elections changed the familiar, once-formidable force of party powerbrokers at the nominating conventions for both the Democrats and the Republicans. Where once the hotel suites of the nominating conventions reigned as the center of the nation's political parties, Democrats and Republicans in the twentieth century now routinely built and financed ever more well-appointed and fully-staffed professional offices, albeit in temporarily rented spaces until the early 1970s. Democrats and Republicans in the early decades of the twentieth century financed their own professional publicity departments and staffed these ever larger, if still temporary, national headquarters and offices in election years. Hotel suites gave way to larger, temporarily rented office suites, and these, in turn, gave way to permanent national headquarters in the 1970s and the 1980s within just a few blocks of each other on Capitol Hill.

Governor William McKinley's 1896 campaign held to the still-familiar campaigning from his home in Canton, Ohio, but Democrat William Jennings Bryan did something no Democrat or Republican had ever done before 1896. Bryan was the first candidate to leave his home and travel by train across the country in 1896 to speak to voters in the campaign. He traveled by train to July's Democratic National Convention in Chicago as the first presidential nominee to ever attend a nominating convention in person, before he set out to travel thousands of miles in the Fall to speak with his thousands of supporters.

It all began when Bryan boarded his 14-car train in Lincoln, Nebraska on Sunday, July 5, 1896 to take him to Chicago's Democratic National Convention, and continued that summer and fall in the Nebraskan's history-making travels in his campaigning.[127] While Bryan traveled by train to speak with tens of thousands of Americans in cities and towns across the country, thousands of Republicans still traveled as customary by train to McKinley's hometown of Canton, Ohio and walked from the town's train station in downtown Canton a few blocks to the Mc-

---

127 "Nebraskans To Boom Bryan." *The New York Times* Monday, July 6, 1896, 3.

Kinley family's home on North Market Ave. Here, they caught a glimpse of Mc-Kinley as he strode out in his yard with its shade trees and wrought-iron fence to greet visitors, what in black-and-white photographs in newspapers, weekly newsmagazines, and all manner of publications became the nation's most famous front-yard that Fall.

Having won the Democratic Party's nomination at its Chicago convention, Nebraska's William Jennings Bryan, a former House member who held his seat for Nebraska's second Congressional District for two terms in the years just before his 1896 campaign, was the first presidential candidate to travel by railroad across the United States in his campaign. Lincoln, Nebraska's railroad station that fall was the scene of regular departures for the Democratic presidential nominee, as Bryan boarded the train in downtown Lincoln and headed out across the country to speak to crowds gathered everywhere from large railyards with many thousands of his supporters to sometimes small groups of only a few dozen supporters crowding together trackside. Wearing his white dress-shirt and his jacket, Bryan held on to the railing on the rear-platforms of his railroad cars and leaned out over the gathered crowds, wearing their own straw-hats, white dress-shirts, and either sporting suspenders or jackets as they stood on the railbeds of the train's tracks to see the first presidential candidate of their lifetimes ever to visit their towns, hear him speak, and maybe have a chance to shake his hand before his train departed to the next town.

On the afternoon of Monday, August 10, 1896, William Jennings Bryan and his travels by train brought him to the hometown of Republican nominee William McKinley. Arriving at the railroad station in downtown Canton that so many of Governor McKinley's supporters had arrived at over the months to walk the short distance to the family's home on North Market Ave., Bryan and his wife, who were traveling on a five-day trip taking them from their home in Nebraska to New York and then back to their home in Lincoln, stopped that Monday in the hometown of their Republican rival as a part of their scheduled itinerary en route to New York City. Bryan's stop in Canton was far shorter than most visitors that fall, as Bryan and his wife didn't even leave the train for their stop in Canton. Instead, Bryan spoke to a crowd of his supporters and to curious Cantonites who turned out to see the Democratic candidate at the train station.[128] "Hats were thrown in the air and the enthusiasm of the crowd was manifest in every conceivable way," *The New York Times* reported from Canton of Bryan's visit.[129] Bryan's

---

128 "Bryan at the Home of McKinley, He is Given a Respectful Hearing and Compliments His Opponent." *The Chicago Daily Tribune* Tuesday, August 11, 1896, 3.
129 "Bryan Talks at Canton, Cheers about Equally Divided between Rival Candidates." *The New York Times* Tuesday, August 11, 1896, 3.

train departed shortly after his speech, giving the Democratic candidate a short time to rest before his next stop to speak to another crowd of some 1,500 supporters in the town of Alliance some 20-miles from Canton.

"Bryan had mastered the science of electioneering by train," Paolo E. Colette tells us of William Jennings Bryan, traveling for days at a time by railroad from his home in Lincoln and then returning to Nebraska after delivering as many as 35 or more speeches a day to railyard crowds who sometimes had spent hours standing near railroad tracks waiting for the Democratic nominee to arrive in their town. The candidate himself, his family, and those elected officials traveling with him stepped out onto the rear-platform of his train and spoke for a time before departing, usually on a tight schedule to make it to the next town and the next speech.[130] In all, Bryan traveled some 18,000 miles by train and visited some 29 states in the fall of 1896, with an itinerary that saw Bryan sometimes roused from his sleep in the middle-of-the-night to awaken and speak when his train arrived in towns, with large crowds waiting at whatever hour it was to have their chance to see the Democratic candidate. Bryan would wake up and speak to these crowds from the train's rear-platform before the train departed with the candidate falling back asleep until the next stop. "Seconds after he was awakened, he would be ready to speak," Coletta says of Bryan, who was able to fall asleep after his middle-of-the-night speeches "in a matter of seconds," either in a chair or stretched out on the floor of his railroad car where he would sleep until being awakened for his next stop and his next speech.

Tuesday, November 3, 1896's election culminated a campaign like no other in the history of the Democrats and Republicans, with the defeat of Bryan by McKinley. Republicans held their House and Senate majorities in that Tuesday's elections, and sent the Democrats reeling from their defeats. Continued majorities for the Republicans in 1898's midterms underscored the difficulties facing the Democrats.

Tuesday, November 6, 1900's reelection of President William McKinley and his Vice-Presidential running mate Theodore Roosevelt was yet another disappointing defeat for the Democrats, who'd renominated Nebraska's William Jennings Bryan at July 1900's Democratic National Convention in Kansas City to his second consecutive ticket for the party. In the months leading up to the 1900 rematch between McKinley and Bryan, the Nebraska Democrat brought the same energy to his travels he'd had in 1896, once again, departing from the train station in his hometown of Lincoln for days at a time to take his campaigning across the country. In 1900's

---

130 Paolo E. Coletta, *William Jennings Bryan: Political Evangelist, 1860–1908.* The University of Nebraska Press, 1964, 174.

campaign, Bryan spoke to tens of thousands of supporters with his travels to more than 17 states. With McKinley's reelection that November, Republicans kept their majorities in the House and Senate. New York's then-Governor Theodore Roosevelt, taking a page from Bryan's playbook, had left the Governor's Mansion behind in Albany to travel across the country and speak as the Republicans' Vice Presidential candidate in person to the American people. It was the first time that a nominee of the Republicans, President or Vice President, traveled around the country to meet and speak with voters. Governor Roosevelt traveled to some 24 states in eight weeks' time in the fall of 1900, speaking to audiences and crowds across the country and, like Bryan, leaning out over the crowds while holding the railing on the rear-platform of his railroad car.

Bryan's successive losses in 1896 and in 1900 disappointed his fellow Democrats, and left little in the way of support for Bryan's nomination to a third ticket at July 1904's Democratic National Convention.[131] Alton Parker defeated his closest Democratic rivals, including famed newspaper publisher and former Representative William Randolph Hearst, on the first ballot at 1904's Democratic National Convention in St. Louis. Parker was picked by the Democrats to take on President Roosevelt, who succeeded to the Presidency with the shooting of President Mc-Kinley in September 1901 less than a year into his second term.[132] Roosevelt's 1904 reelection playbook was familiar to Democratic and Republican sitting Presidents over the years, staying mostly in Washington, D.C. and at his family home in Oyster Bay, with nothing like Roosevelt's whirlwind travels by train across the country in 1900 as the Republican's Vice-Presidential nominee just four years earlier.

"Roosevelt Sweeps North and West and Is Elected President," *The New York Times* headlines reported Wednesday morning, November 9, 1904, the morning after Roosevelt's reelection with a win of 32 states stretching from Maine to California. "Says He Will Not Run Again," the *Times*' headline told readers that morning, telling the world what the President had told some 50 or so reporters only hours earlier that previous evening as White House reporters were asked to gather

---

131 "Bryan the Idol Smashed by Party, Former Leader on Eighth Anniversary of His Triumph Repudiated by Vote of 647 to 299, Magic Power is Gone, Test Forced by Nebraskan Served to Show how Strong the Parker Sentiment has Grown." *The Chicago Daily Tribune* Friday, July 8, 1904, 1.

132 "Parker Chosen on First Ballot, Democrats Nominated New York Judge on Platform Agreed to Without any Opposition, Bryan to Support Him, Result is not Reached until Early Hour this Morning and After Much Oratory." *The Chicago Daily Tribune* Saturday, July 9, 1904, 1.

together by the President for a brief statement.[133] "Under no circumstances will I be a candidate for or accept another nomination," the President said to the surprised reporters in the White House at 10 o'clock in the evening, and to more than a few of the President's own staff who also heard the announcement with the same surprise. Years later, Roosevelt himself expressed his regret for what he sometimes called his "reckless pledge," yet that regret was by every measure less important to the President than the regret Roosevelt felt for the performance of the administration of his friend and fellow Republican President William Howard Taft. Taft's administration was viewed unhappily by Roosevelt from his retirement, setting up in 1912 one of the most precedent-shattering chapters in the history of presidential elections.

"The Administration has certainly wholly failed in keeping the party in substantial [unity], and what I mind most is that the revolt is not merely among the political leaders but among the masses of the people," Theodore Roosevelt said in July 1910 of his onetime friend President William Howard Taft, expressing his disappointment that President Taft had done too little to hold the Republicans together in the months before 1910's midterm defeats.[134] Democrats rallied in 1910's midterms to win their first House majority in almost two decades, blame placed squarely on the shoulders of Taft by Roosevelt.[135]

By the spring of 1911, Roosevelt kept up his busy schedule traveling the country and speaking before audiences, as well as talking off-the-cuff and on-the-record with newspaper reporters. Roosevelt spoke on a wide range of issues to audiences across the country in the year after 1910's midterm losses. He spoke variously of his proposals on economic and financial matters, his support for the ratification of an Amendment to the Constitution for the direct election of members of the Senate, and his thoughts on any number of other issues of the day. The former President, too, expressed his interest and support of the new presidential primaries being adopted and put into place in California, Nebraska, Oregon, Wisconsin, and other states, states also adopting and innovating ways for voters in these states to have a say through initiatives, recalls, referendums, and other such reforms.

Wednesday, February 21, 1912's "my hat is in the ring" pledge delivered by Roosevelt before a crowd in at the railroad station in downtown Cleveland was in

---

133 "Roosevelt Sweeps North and West and is Elected President, Says He will not Run Again, Will have 325 Electoral Votes, Republican Gains in Congress, Folk, LaFollette, and Douglas win Governorship Fights." *The New York Times* Wednesday, November 9, 1904, 1.

134 George E. Mowry, "Theodore Roosevelt and the Election of 1910." *The Mississippi Valley Historical Review* 25, no. 4, March 1939, 525.

135 Kenneth C. Martis, *The Historical Atlas of the Political Parties in the United States Congress, 1789 – 1989.* Macmillan Publishing Company, 1989, 165.

every respect the most precedent-setting and precedent-shattering decision by a former President, taking on his own party's sitting President in the newly-created primary contests. With thirteen Republican presidential primary elections scheduled that Spring, Roosevelt and Taft took to the railroads with these clashes starting with Tuesday, March 19, 1912's North Dakota primary. Democrats held 12 such primaries in these same states – except New York – in Democratic contests that featured then-Governor Woodrow Wilson facing Missouri's Champ Clark. President Taft's losses in nine of these thirteen state contests angered and embarrassed the Taft White House and energized Roosevelt's supporters, some of whom now took to calling themselves the Insurgents.

President Taft's loss in Tuesday, May 21, 1912's Ohio primary was especially difficult for President Taft, who campaigned across his home state in some cases with Taft speaking in the same towns on the same day that Roosevelt's own train either had already arrived earlier or would arrive sometime later bringing the former President to speak to these same Ohioans.[136] Never in the history of the United States had a sitting President traveled by train to defend their record and ask for the support of their party's voters. The train of the sitting President and the train of the former President traveling through the same Ohio towns on the same days to speak to voters was wholly without precedent for Democrats or Republicans.[137] Losses in his home state of Ohio and eight other states with presidential primaries left President Taft embarrassed and his own party reeling, yet with only 278 delegates, Roosevelt's likelihood of replacing a sitting President with the backing of Senators, Representatives, Governors, and others seemed impossible.

Wednesday, June 19, 1912's renomination of President Taft on the first ballot by delegates at the Republican National Convention came as a disappointment to Roosevelt's backers, even as expected as the outcome was considering the support of the party's power-brokers for President Taft. President Taft was easily nominated for November's ticket, even as hundreds of Roosevelt's delegates on the convention floor and supporters in the audience in the Chicago Coliseum yelled "We Want Teddy." Fistfights and scuffles broke out between supporters loyal to President Taft and those supporting Roosevelt as delegates at the Chicago Coliseum spilled

---

136 "Roosevelt Triumphant in Ohio, Claims 15 Districts out of the 21, Harmon Wins, two to one, from Wilson, Colonel's Vote 59,054 to Taft's 41,435 with One-Fourth of Returns in, Taft Carries Cincinnati, but Cleveland, which Senator Burton Hoped to Win for Him, Goes to Roosevelt, Taft Men Claim Half, Declare Roosevelt Estimate Exaggerated but Give out No Figures, Fight Won, says Roosevelt, Gets the News at Oyster Bay and Beams with Delight at His Victory." *The New York Times* Wednesday, May 22, 1912, 1.

137 William Manners, *TR and Will: A Friendship that Split the Republican Party.* Harcourt, Brace and World, 1969, 229.

out onto the sidewalks of South Wabash Ave. Roosevelt huddled for a time with his advisors in his temporary headquarters on the second floor of Chicago's Congress Hotel to discuss his next move. The former President left little doubt that he was still prepared to carry his message to the country's voters in November.

"I went before the people, and I won," Roosevelt said, speaking to a large audience of his supporters at almost two o'clock in the morning on Thursday, June 20, 1912. "Let's find out whether the Republican Party is still the party of the plain people, the people of the United States, or the party of the bosses, and the professional politicians acting in the interests of special privilege," Roosevelt said. In their speeches, Roosevelt and Gov. Johnson both spoke against the Republican Party's old-guard and its bosses and prepared their supporters for a party-splitting bolt in the fall. "We are prepared for the birth of a new Republican Party which will nominate President Theodore Roosevelt," Johnson told Roosevelt's supporters that Thursday morning. "This new party will be an honest party," Johnson told the crowd.[138]

Days later, on Saturday evening, June 22, 1912, as their exhausted supporters, christened the Bolters by some newspaper reporters, prepared to leave the week's bedlam in Chicago and return to their homes, Roosevelt and Johnson spoke again to their supporters meeting in Chicago's Orchestra Hall, about a mile from the Coliseum where the Republican National Convention was adjourning. Supporters of Roosevelt met for one last time in Chicago before they returned home, urged to begin preparations for a Fall presidential election like none ever seen and promising to return to Chicago in August for another convention. "If you wish me to make the fight, I will make it, even if only one state should support me," Roosevelt said to his supporters in Orchestra Hall before their return home on the evening of Saturday, June 22, 1912. "The only condition I impose is that you shall feel entirely free when you come together to substitute any other man in my place if you deem it better for the movement, and in such case I will give him my heartiest support."[139] Roosevelt and Johnson both urged their supporters to travel

---

138 "Roosevelt, Beaten, to Bolt Today, Gives the Word in Early Morning, Taft's Nomination Seems Assured, Many of Colonel's Delegates will not Follow Him from Convention, Compromise Talk, Too, Taft Strength Grows, Yesterday's Vote, 564 to 510, Believed to Represent the Actual Line-Up, Woman Leads Cheering, Starts a Demonstration for the Colonel that Lasts Almost an Hour, Hadley Shares in it, Root Quells Disorder, Proves a Firm Chairman, but There is a Great Deal of Confusion During the Speeches." *The New York Times* Thursday, June 20, 1912, 1.

139 "Roosevelt Delegates Go from the Regular to Rump Convention, Gov. Johnson Presides, Scores the National Committee as Thieves and Promises them a Lesson, New Party on Ruins of Old, Pendergast Makes the Nominating Speech He Had Prepared for Regular Convention, Commandment as Platform, It is 'Thou Shalt Not Steal,' Applied to All the Affairs of Life, Wife and Daughters There,

back home and "sound out the country," and prepare to return in a few weeks to Chicago to nominate a new national ticket. "Here is the birth of a new party," Johnson told his supporters, leaving little if any doubt as to what would take shape in the coming days as the flurry of meetings and work back home in their states prepared them for the National Progressive Convention later in August.

With the Democratic National Convention, the National Progressive Convention, and the Republican National Convention all finished by August 1912, voters across the United States had the extraordinary opportunity for the first time to see a sitting President campaign by automobile and by train in their cities and towns. As War Secretary, William Howard Taft traveled the country in the fall of 1908 as a cabinet member and candidate when campaigning against Democrat William Jennings Bryan, but now in the fall of 1912 as the first sitting President in the history of the United States to travel by railroad and automobile across parts of the United States, Taft brought the President himself to cities and towns across the country. For the first time, Americans could see the President of the United States at their town's train station or standing in the rear of a convertible in their own or talking from the steps of a nearby tenement building pleading for votes.

Traveling the country by trains and speaking to crowds gathered alongside the tracks at train stations, in switching yards, and wherever else their trains stopped to speak to crowds from the now-familiar perch of their rear-car platforms, President William Howard Taft, Woodrow Wilson, and former President Theodore Roosevelt brought presidential campaigning to the people. They forever changed the campaigning of presidential candidates for the Democrats and Republicans in the fall of 1912, even as the front-porch tradition held for at least a few more presidential elections still in the twentieth century. Iconic black-and-white photographs of Roosevelt, Taft, and Wilson leaning over the railings of the platforms on the rear-car of their trains endure across the ages from the first campaign to date in the nation's history when travel took on an importance in presidential elections. When Roosevelt was shot and seriously wounded in Milwaukee, Wisconsin on Monday, October 14, 1912, during a visit to that city, it came in the closing weeks of a frenetic fall of travel for Roosevelt, Taft, and Wilson.[140] In the end, as expected,

---

News that Bolting Convention was to be Held Drew a Great Crowd and the Police Reserves." *The New York Times* Sunday, June 23, 1912, 7.

140 "Maniac in Milwaukee Shoots Col. Roosevelt, He Ignores Wound, Speaks an Hour, Goes to Hospital, Would-Be Assassin is John Schrank, Once Saloonkeeper Here, a Maniac on Third Term, Obsessed with Belief That He was Commissioned to Remove Peril to Nation, Had Dream of McKinley, Martyred President, He Says, Told Him that Roosevelt Had Him Slain, Started on Colonel's Trail, Went South after Buying Revolver and Followed Ex-President Closely, Was Baffled in Chicago,

the Republican rift eased the path for Wilson and the Democrats to win the White House. Democrats held their majority in the House that Tuesday and carried a Senate majority, winning the White House and both chambers of Congress for the first time since President Grover Cleveland in 1892.

President Woodrow Wilson's narrowest of reelection bids to a second term facing former Associate Supreme Court Justice Charles Evans Hughes, who stepped down from the bench in June 1916 to accept the nomination of the Republican National Convention, was to some extent a measure of the closeness that 1912's election would have been had it not been for Roosevelt's Progressive bolt. Had Republican Charles Evans Hughes carried California in 1916's election, which President Wilson carried by fewer than 3,800 votes, Hughes would have been elected with 267 Electoral votes to 264 for Wilson.[141] Northeastern and midwestern states from New England through the Upper Midwest and the Great Lakes – torn in two by Roosevelt's Progressive ticket in November 1912 – returned to the Republicans in 1916's contest. Wilson managed to win reelection to his second term by winning most of the Great Plains, Mountain and Western states as well as the solidly Democratic South, but Wilson lost his home state of New Jersey and its neighbor New York to the Associate Supreme Court Justice who'd taken to the nation's rails to speak by rear-platform train-station and rail-yard speeches along with President Wilson and his own travels that fall. The era of candidate travel in presidential elections had arrived for good by 1916, and elections of the President would never be the same again.

In Tuesday, November 2, 1920's election, Democrats and Republicans alike stuck closely to a shared playbook of campaigning, in nominating their national tickets with candidates from the must-win state of Ohio. Senator Warren Harding of Marion faced Governor James M. Cox, Sr. of Dayton in that year's November race. Cox's Vice-Presidential running mate, Franklin Roosevelt, filled out the fall ticket for the Democrats. Together, the Governor of Ohio and New York's Roosevelt campaigned by train at a busy pace, the black-and-white photographs of the Democratic nominees campaigning by train across the country familiar to readers of the nation's newspapers and weekly newsmagazines. Senator Harding, too, traveled by train across the country in the closing months of 1920's race, even as the Republican ticket made the most of mass-marketing Mount Vernon Avenue as one of the last bids of the disappearing era of front-porch presidential campaigns in the country's history.

Then He Went Early to Milwaukee and Planned Carefully to Make Sure of His Victim." *The New York Times* Tuesday, October 15, 1912, 1.

141 Neal R. Peirce, *The People's President: The Electoral College in American History and the Direct Vote Alternative.* Simon and Schuster, 1968, 321.

In the fall of 1920, there was no more familiar front-porch and front-yard in the United States than the home of Warren Harding on Mount Vernon Ave. in Marion, with the family's porch looking out on the tree-lined street where the Ohio Senator spoke each day delivering speeches to visiting crowds, the kind of campaigning that now seemed to be as much of throwback for headlines and well-staged photographs in morning newspapers and weekly newsmagazines. From the train station in downtown Marion, group after group made their way to Mount Vernon Avenue. Black-and-white motion picture newsreels of visitors standing on the lawn of the Harding family in Marion and greeting the Senator standing on the steps of his home were shown coast-to-coast in movie theaters, the last campaign of its kind with visitors traveling a distance to the hometown of the candidate instead of the candidates traveling themselves to the cities and towns of voters.

As Americans were entertained weekly with a new generation of actresses and actors in the feature silent motion-picture films of the day, the summer and fall of 1920 featured newsreels of some of these same actresses and actors filmed visiting the Harding home in the newsreels that played between their feature motion-pictures in hundreds of theaters across the country. "Get the Hook for Dems, Al Jolson Sings to Harding, Theater Stars Chase Care at Marion Jubilee," *The Chicago Daily Tribune*'s Wednesday, August 25, 1920, headline told its readers.[142] Organized by Al Jolson, actresses and actors including Douglas Fairbanks, Mary Pickford, Ethel Barrymore, Lillian Gish, and Pearl White, all gathered on the steps of the Harding home. Jolson led his famous entourage of more than 70 actresses and actors arriving by a special charter train as a part of the Harding and Coolidge Theatrical League. Jolson, Fairbanks, Pickford, and Barrymore were among those actresses and actors lending their talent and their time to appearing on the steps of the Harding porch and in the popular black-and-white newsreels fitted in between the feature silent films starring these same actresses and actors.

Thousands of Marion's residents and out-of-town visitors came to the town's Lincoln Park stadium to watch their local team, the Kerrigan Tailors, play an exhibition game with the Chicago Cubs on Thursday, September 2, 1920, as one of the Madison Ave.-style marketing bids by the Republicans that fall. Senator Harding's "busy morning on the front porch and a happy afternoon at the ball field," as *The Chicago Daily Tribune* reported, featured the kind of well-scripted orchestration and theatrics that Republicans publicized that fall.[143] Cubs pitcher Grover Cleve-

---

142 "Get the Hook for Dems, Al Jolson Sings to Harding, Theater Stars Chase Care at Marion Jubilee." *The Chicago Daily Tribune* Wednesday, August 25, 1920, 9.
143 "Harding Drives a Few Homers for 'Cub' Guests, Against One Man Team in World League." *The Chicago Daily Tribune* Friday, September 3, 1920, 2.

land Alexander led his teammates to a three to one victory over the Tailors that Thursday with a crowd of some 7,000 fans in the stands. Harding, *The New York Times* tells us, "slipped on a glove and caught a dozen passes from Grover Cleveland Alexander." "And he caught every ball," the *Times* said of then-Senator Harding, "although Alexander didn't use his wicked twirls, but it was good for the movies."[144] Meanwhile, the Democratic ticket saw Ohio's Governor and his running mate take their campaigns to many of these same Main Streets across the Midwest and elsewhere that fall as travel by train for presidential candidates grew even more commonplace for many Americans.

Side-by-side headlines in *The Chicago Daily Tribune* on Friday morning, September 3, 1920, tell the story of the Democratic and Republican tickets in the fall of 1920. "Harding Drives a Few Homers for 'Cub' Guests," headlines in the *Tribune* reported on that previous day's baseball game between the Cubs and Marion's Kerrigan Tailors.[145] "Cox Starts 10,000 Mile Speaking Tour of West, In Michigan Today, in Chicago Sunday," the *Tribune*'s headline right next to the headline from Marion told readers in its reporting with Governor Cox at the capitol in Columbus on his upcoming travels by train ("one of the longest stumping tours ever undertaken by a presidential nominee," the *Tribune* noted) that same Friday morning.[146]

"Cox to Start Next Week," *The New York Times*' headlines reported weeks earlier on Tuesday, August 24, 1920, of one of Cox's longest campaign trips that fall by train to the Midwest and the West, a tour taking him across the country for almost a full month's travels through 20 different states with the delivery of more than 100 speeches. "Tour of West to be Most Extensive of any Presidential Nominee," the *Times* told its readers.[147] While Harding spoke to visitors from his tree-shaded porch in Marion and spent hours off-the-record with newspaper reporters in the family's backyard in a small bungalow set aside by the Harding's for reporters to spend their days during the fall's campaign, Cox and Roosevelt traveled the

---

144 "Harding Demands Team Government, Tells Chicago Cubs 'One-Man Team' Muffed and Struck Out in Paris, They Play Game in Marion, Nominee Refuses Plea of Delegation of Teachers, Confers with Senator Knox." *The New York Times* Friday, September 3, 1920, 3.

145 "Harding Drives a Few Homers for 'Cub' Guests, Against One Man Team in World League." *The Chicago Daily Tribune* Friday, September 3, 1920, 2.

146 "Cox Starts 10,000 Mile Speaking Tour of West, In Michigan Today, in Chicago Sunday." *The Chicago Daily Tribune* Friday, September 3, 1920, 2.

147 "Cox to Start Next Week, Tour of West to be Most Extensive of any Presidential Nominee." *The New York Times* Tuesday, August 24, 1920, 3. *The New York Times* noted that for this trip in August, Governor Cox and his traveling party were in three railroad cars that included the 20 or so reporters and silent motion-picture newsreel crews. Cox's private car was equipped, *The New York Times* told its readers, with a microphone and speakers ("a sound amplifying device") that allowed the candidate to be heard some 250 feet or more from the rear-platform of the train.

country, shaking hands in crowds, riding in automobiles at parades, appearing together at state fairs and other events and speaking to crowds from the rear-platform of their trains, with Cox traveling some 22,000 miles by train that fall. That fall, Harding finally left the quiet of Marion for several different trips by train across the Midwest in the closing weeks of the fall 1920's contest. Harding made some 100 speeches in travels taking him to Illinois, Indiana, Iowa, Kentucky, Missouri, New York, and Oklahoma.

Tuesday, November 2, 1920's election capped a historic race for the Republicans, with President-elect Warren Harding and Vice President-elect Calvin Coolidge preparing for their administration with Republican majorities in the House and in the Senate. Will Rogers' well-remembered quip – "I don't belong to any organized political faith, I am a Democrat" – spoke to the difficulties facing the Democrats.[148] Republicans governed with confidence, even in the face of White House scandal. Republicans held their Congressional majorities in 1922's midterms, but Democrats confounded expectations and won some 75 seats in the House of Representatives and six seats in the Senate, not enough for a majority but enough to let the country know that the Democrats had not been entirely routed.[149] Still, Democrats' dim prospects for returning to the White House and their difficulty holding their own in the House and Senate invoked comparisons of the Democrats to the disagreements and disorganization of the nineteenth century's Whigs.

June 1924's Republican National Convention in Cleveland and New York City's Democratic National Convention later that month at Madison Square Garden were the first national conventions to be carried on the airwaves of commercial networks covering most of the Eastern United States and large parts of the Midwest. "It was Coolidge, Coolidge all the way," *The New York Times* told its readers from Cleveland's convention that June, proceedings heard by radio listeners at home in the first national nominating convention carried by radio's commercial stations and their growing listening audiences reaching Americans in the quiet of their homes.[150] Speeches and programming of all kinds filled the airwaves from Cleveland's convention. Only missing still from Cleveland and New York City were the voices of the candidates themselves. Candidates still did not attend their conven-

148 Richard D. White, Jr., *Will Rogers: A Political Life.* Texas Tech University Press, 2011, 65.
149 David Burner, *The Politics of Provincialism: The Democratic Party in Transition, 1918–1932.* Alfred A. Knopf, 1970, 104.
150 "Convention Cheers Keynote Attack on Congress, and Praise of Coolidge, Who Dominates the Session, Leaders Hold Night Conference on Second Place, Back Coolidge, says Burton, He Arraigns Legislators in Panegyric of the President, Galleries Voice Approval, League's Court is Upheld, and Coolidge Declared Right in all Clashes with Congress, Third of Seats Empty." *The New York Times* Wednesday, June 11, 1924, 1.

tions in person, and wouldn't do so for another decade or longer. Coolidge listened by radio from the White House in Washington, D.C. like millions of his fellow Americans to the broadcasts of the Republican National Convention, while the Democratic contenders for that party's nomination were just as well not there in person to see firsthand the mess that ensued in New York's Madison Square Garden, an embarrassing moment for the Democrats as the two-thirds nomination rule turned Madison Square Garden into a national embarrassment for those Democrats tuning in at home on their radios.

With the first ballot cast in Madison Square Garden on Monday, June 30, 1924, Democratic delegates began the longest, most difficult nominating convention since Charleston's April 1860 debacle. New York's then-Governor Al Smith and Wilson's Treasury Secretary William McAdoo became household names to large numbers of radio listeners as the leading contenders for the Democratic nomination, with West Virginia's John W. Davis, a prominent Wall Street attorney, Senator Oscar Underwood of Alabama, Senator Carter Class of Lynchburg, Virginia and several others also winning the ballots of some of the 1,089 delegates in Madison Square Garden. By the end of that Monday evening, Democratic delegates had cast some 15 inconclusive ballots, falling short of the 726 delegates needed under the two-thirds nomination rule to select 1924s national ticket. That Monday's 15 votes bewildered Americans listening at home in contrast to the calm of Cleveland's Republican National Convention only a few weeks earlier. What happened that Monday, June 30, 1924 was only the first day of a 17-day convention that soon descended into an embarrassing stalemate.[151] "A nation listening in to a convention by radio for the first time was entertained and embittered," historian David Burner tells us in 1970's definitive *The Politics of Provincialism: The Democratic Party in Transition, 1918 – 1932*.[152] Democrats by turns seemed incapable of settling their disagreements and disinterested in the damage being done as the drawn-out balloting and drawling hours of debates could be heard in the quiet of homes across the country listening to their radios late into the night and often into the early-morning hours.

---

151 "McAdoo Ahead on Fifteenth Ballot with 479, Smith 305, Governor gains 64 during Day to his Rival's 47, J.W. Davis Third with 61, Adjourn to 10:30 A.M. Today, Battle Lines hold Firm, McAdoo and Smith Fail to Reach Victory in Day of Balloting, Each makes Small Gains, John W. Davis Advances Steadily, His Strength may be Tested Today, 17 Still in the Contest, Silzer of New Jersey, Sweet of Colorado, Kendrick of Wyoming, and Ferris of Michigan Quit." *The New York Times* Tuesday, July 1, 1924, 1.
152 David Burner, *The Politics of Provincialism: The Democratic Party in Transition, 1918 – 1932*. Alfred A. Knopf, 1970, 115.

At the end of the convention's first day on Monday, June 30, 1924, 15 ballots had been cast by delegates. Two days later, in a speech to delegates in Madison Square Garden on Wednesday, July 2, 1924, William Jennings Bryan took the stage and faced not only heckling from Smith's supporters during his broadcast, but also frustrated broadcast technicians who'd drawn a chalk box on the stage for Bryan's benefit so he knew where to stand for the microphones carrying his words to listeners at home. Instead of standing in the chalk-drawn box for his words to be carried by microphones clearly to the radio listening audience, Bryan paced back and forth across the Madison Square Garden stage, hanging out over the railing to address the audience in the Garden like the rear-platforms of the trains he'd crisscrossed the country in three different presidential races, causing the radio listening audience to be unable to hear large portions of his remarks.[153] That next day, on Thursday, July 3, 1924, Democratic delegates cast their fifty-seventh ballot to tie the record set in April 1860 in Charleston, as delegates dug in their heels for their respective candidates and showed no sign of adjourning without a fall ticket.

With another 19 ballots cast by delegates on the floor of Madison Square Garden on Thursday, July 3, 1924 – including the fifty-seventh ballot that Thursday evening surpassing the historic mark from April 1860's Charleston convention, delegates kept their roll-call ballots with little change for the candidates from ballot-to-ballot. Delegates backing California's McAdoo began pressing the convention to recess for several weeks, and then reconvene either in Kansas City or Washington, D.C. or elsewhere.[154] With no support to adjourn, the convention's eighty-seventh ballot was cast late in the evening of Monday, July 7, 1924, as Governor Smith's delegates had a slight lead over McAdoo and other candidates, but still short of the two-thirds of the delegates needed for the nomination.

Tuesday, July 8, 1924 finally brought the 17-day embarrassment for Democrats to a close with the announcement by New York's Governor that he would urge delegates withdraw his name if delegates for the former Treasury Secretary did the same. Confusion spread through state delegations on the floor of Madison Square Garden, as word went through the delegations that either West Virginia's Davis or Senator Glass might head the fall's national ticket. Franklin Roosevelt, a manager for Gov. Smith, took to the podium to make his announcement. "For the good of the party, Governor Smith authorizes me to say that immediately after Mr. McAdoo

153 "How Delegates Took Bryan's Speech, Turmoil and Disorder Prevails, As He Attempts to Push McAdoo, New York Group is Quiet, But Interrupters Were Plenty in Other State Delegations." *The New York Times* Thursday, July 3, 1924, 3.
154 "McAdoo Men Suggest Meeting Elsewhere, Talk of Asking for Adjournment to Another City if Deadlock Keeps Up." *The New York Times* Friday, July 4, 1924, 2.

withdraws, Governor Smith will withdraw his name," Roosevelt told the convention late that Tuesday evening, July 8, 1924, just before the delegates took their ninety-fourth ballot.[155] Another four ballots were taken by delegates on the floor of Madison Square Garden as confusion continued among state delegation and in the conversations and closed-door meetings taking place. Finally, in the early-morning hours of Wednesday, July 9, 1924, at around 2:45 A.M., McAdoo's camp released a statement from their suite at the Madison Square Hotel withdrawing his name from the running after the ninety-ninth ballot taken by the delegates, a ninety-ninth ballot with an almost evenly split number of delegates between Smith and McAdoo with a substantial number of delegates now casting their ballots for West Virginia's Davis. As the news of McAdoo's statement made its way through the delegates on the floor and in the galleries of Madison Square Garden, one final ballot, the convention's one hundredth ballot, was taken at almost four o'clock in the morning, after which delegates agreed to adjourn until noon later that day.

"Davis Is Put over in Wild Stampede," *The New York Times*' front-page headlines told readers on Thursday morning, July 10, 1924. "Weary Delegates Jump for Band Wagon and Then All Join Big Demonstration."[156] When the convention reconvened midday Wednesday with a one hundred first and one hundred second ballot as the last deadlocked ballots cast that afternoon, West Virginia's Davis was finally selected on the one hundred third and final ballot around 3:30 in the afternoon on Wednesday, July 9, 1924. After 17-days of the Democratic National Convention's deadlock broadcast live to listening audiences up and down the East Coast and across the Midwest, the nomination of Davis revealed the enormous risks of embarrassment for Democrats and Republicans with the arrival of radio's unseen but vast listening audiences.

Determined to avoid a second deadlocked nomination, Democrats meeting in Houston, Texas for June 1928's Democratic National Convention selected New York's then-Governor Al Smith on the first ballot at their June convention, "astounding in contrast to the previous convention," historian David Burner tells us, "the Democrats behaved like an assembly of Republicans."[157] In keeping with the custom of nominees still not attending the national nominating conventions

---

155 "Thrills Come Early in Morning after Session Opens Tamely, Galleries Cheer Steadfast Stand of Smith Supporters and Boo Unyielding McAdoo States, 'Dark Horses' Make Gains after Ralston Goes." *The New York Times* Wednesday, July 9, 1924, 1.
156 "Davis Is Put over in Wild Stampede, Weary Delegates Jump for Band Wagon and Then All Join Big Demonstration, It Is West Virginia's Day, Convention Pays Tribute to the Men and the State that Gave It the New Leader." *The New York Times* Thursday, July 10, 1924, 1.
157 David Burner, *The Politics of Provincialism: The Democratic Party in Transition, 1918 – 1932.* Alfred A. Knopf, 1970, 192 – 193.

in person, New York's Governor accepted his nomination from the statehouse in Albany on Tuesday, August 21, 1928 while Herbert Hoover thanked his fellow Republicans and accepted their nomination from his home in Palo Alto, California.[158] Facing off in the fall, Gov. Smith and Secretary of Commerce Hoover fought on every-front in a campaign tinged by the anti-Catholic, anti-alcohol, anti-immigrant, and anti-urban sentiments, not to mention continuing appeals to the popular figures of Hollywood and professional athletes for Democrats and Republicans alike.

Photographed after winning their third straight World Series game against the Cardinals at St. Louis' Sportsman's Park on Monday, October 8, 1928 in a series they'd sweep in four-games that next day, the New York Yankees including Babe Ruth and Lou Gehrig stood smiling on the field at Sportsman's Park holding FOR AL SMITH placards.[159] Speaking from the rear-platform of the Yankees' charter-train on Wednesday, October 10, 1928 as it rolled back from St. Louis to New York City, Ruth's exasperation – "if that's the way you feel, to hell with you," Ruth bellowed to one crowd of 2,000 people in Terre Haute, Indiana greeting the Yankee outfielder's praise of Gov. Smith from the train's rear-platform with silence – with the unenthusiastic reception of crowds to his words of support for Gov. Smith spoke to the undercurrents roiling America in the fall of 1928.

In the weeks that followed, both New York's Governor and former Commerce Secretary Herbert Hoover nominated by the Republicans took to the nation's railways to reach the American people, in a campaign where both the radio and railroads brought campaigning almost to the doorsteps of millions of American fam-

---

158 "Hoover Formally Notified, Voices Issues, Opposes Dry Law Repeal or Nullification, Favors Hundreds of Millions for Farm Aid, 70,000 Flock to Stadium, Nominee Addresses the Nation Through Radio in Ceremony at Stanford, Sees Prohibition Abuses, Fact Finding Inquiry to Correct Them Proposed, Republican Tariff is Lauded, Intolerance is Denounced, League Cooperation Favored, Tribute to Coolidge as a Great President." *The New York Times* Sunday, August 12, 1928, 1.
159 Several versions of the photograph – taken for the International Newsreel Corp. at St. Louis' Sportsman's Park on Monday, October 8, 1928 – survive to this day. The reverse of one of these International Newsreel photos with the Al Smith signs reads, "Photo shows left to right, Benny Bengough, Waite Hoyt, Lou Gehrig, Tony Lazzeri, Joe Dugan, Mark Koenig, Bob Meusel, Earl Combs, Babe Ruth and Eddie Bennett, mascot, all members of the New York Yankees, who are rabid Smith fans." Ruth appeared in photographs with Gov. Smith in the fall of 1928 – including a famous photo with Ruth wearing a "Vote for AL SMITH" lapel-card – in a derby-hat and chewing on a cigar. Monday, October 8, 1928's photo of the Yankees in St. Louis also appeared on an iconic colorful "Champions of the World! Champions of Al Smith" campaign poster – with other athletes and coaches ("Be a Good Sport and Vote for Al") including Notre Dame's Knute Rockne and boxer Gene Tunney. Leigh Montville's *The Big Bam: The Life and Times of Babe Ruth* tells the story of Ruth's exasperation with the crowd in Terre Haute, Indiana. Leigh Montville, *The Big Bam: The Life and Times of Babe Ruth*. Doubleday, 2006, 279.

ilies for both Democrats and Republicans in the run-up to 1928's election.[160] Smith and Hoover's trains were fully equipped with everything the candidates and their families and staff needed to speak by radio to the nation's radio listeners and to speak to large crowds from the rear-platforms of their trains in town after town and city after city, reaching larger numbers of voters than ever with coverage by the coast-to-coast radio networks with their large listening audiences, as well as, the motion picture newsreel companies whose cameras and microphones brought the words of the candidates to millions more in the theaters of large cities and small towns alike.

Tuesday, November 6, 1928's election of President-elect Herbert Hoover over New York's Governor Al Smith is well-understood in hindsight as a defeat for the Democrats, where the Democrats won by losing. In 1928's election, Hoover won 40 states and 444 Electoral votes to Smith's eight states, including his six in the solidly-Democratic South and Massachusetts and Rhode Island carried by Gov. Smith with just 87 Electoral votes. But in losing 1928's election in such a sweeping loss, Smith's defeat was one of the most consequential losses in the twentieth century keeping the Democrats distant from the White House when the economy's bottom fell out in a year's time.

"Chicago Listens to Returns Via Radio, Telephone," *The Chicago Daily Tribune*'s Wednesday morning, November 7, 1928, headlines told its readers the morning after Hoover's election. "Voice from Ether Spells End of Former Crowds."[161] In its easily overlooked story located on the upper-left hand of the *Tribune*'s page nine that Wednesday morning, the paper wrote, in so many words, the obituary of a political way of life for millions of Americans now disappearing if not already

---

160 "The well-meaning Democrats of the United States loaded the baggage cars of my 1928 campaign train with every sort of present from pipes, tobacco, clothing, and underwear, to animals, such as large dogs and even a live donkey meant to represent the Democratic emblem," New York's then-Governor Smith later said of his train that traveled across the country in the late summer and fall of 1928 – including as many as 40 newspaper and newsmagazine reporters accompanying the Governor and his family on their travels. Alfred E. Smith, *The Citizen and His Government*. Harper and Brothers, 1935, 129. As for radio, Smith's campaign in the fall of 1928 faced its own difficulties. "Over the radio, then a new and impressive contribution to presidential campaigns, Smith's voice could be heard only with difficulty, for he spoke indistinctly and insisted on dashing from one side of the microphone to the other. His speeches themselves lacked grace and symmetry. He employed 'ain't' and 'he don't' and changed 'work' to 'woik"...His language, gestures, and physical appearance, all of which the new motion-picture newsreels conveyed, stamped him as an intruder in national politics." David Burner, *The Politics of Provincialism: The Democratic Party in Transition, 1918–1932*. Alfred A. Knopf, 1970, 210.
161 "Chicago Listens to Returns Via Radio, Telephone, Voice from Ether Spells End of Former Crowds." *The Chicago Daily Tribune* Wednesday, November 7, 1928, 9.

gone. No longer did crowds swell the sidewalks outside of great metropolitan papers like *The Chicago Daily Tribune* and others in moments of revelry, awaiting the latest election returns from across the country. Now, like the candidates themselves who sat in their family rooms and parlors with their families and their friends awaiting the latest news on their radios, so too did millions upon millions of Americans who now stayed at home on the evening of Tuesday, November 6, 1928, awaiting the breaking news to come to them. Americans cast their votes during the day in their precincts and then came home in the evening to the quiet of their apartments, farmhouse kitchens, and family rooms of their homes where they tuned in their radios to await the latest news. Radio, it seemed, had taken politics indoors. Commercial broadcast stations became up-to-the-minute source of news to far outstrip the once-dominant morning and afternoon papers that, in another day, swayed allegiances on election day with their editorials and their endorsements. But in that Wednesday morning, November 7, 1928 headline in *The Chicago Daily Tribune*, its reporting of the smaller crowds on the streets of Chicago told the larger story of a nation's changing campaigning for the Democrats and the Republicans whose elected officials, candidates, and voters were about to face their greatest challenge in the twentieth century.

Chapter 5 The Democratic and Republican Parties in the New Deal Era and After, 1932 – 1976

"We can save the expense of bringing people here from all over the country later," Governor Franklin Roosevelt said on Friday, July 1, 1932 as he and his family at the Governor's Mansion in Albany celebrated the news of the hour from the Chicago, and got the word quickly back to the Democratic National Convention's mangers still in Chicago Stadium not to adjourn the convention yet. Delegates at the convention had selected Roosevelt to head their ticket and finished their work. Under normal circumstances, they'd be adjourning and returning to their hotel rooms to begin packing for their travels back home. As telephones rang throughout the night that Friday at the mansion and as well-wishers visited Roosevelt to express their congratulations, the Governor and his staff busily worked out the final details of a morning flight from Albany.

With the news that Friday night of the Governor's nomination, the Roosevelt family expressed their gratitude and thanks from Albany to the delegates in Chicago who'd cast their fourth and final ballot for Roosevelt to head the Democratic Party's 1932 ticket. Roosevelt celebrated that evening, surrounded by family and friends and some of his closest aides, all of whom were well-aware that the Republicans would stop at nothing to defeat the Governor that fall in a presidential race whose outcome was far from certain even with the financial calamity that faced the nation. In that moment, Roosevelt did something extraordinary, fully in keeping with the energy he'd promised to bring to the fall campaign. By telephone to Democratic managers in Chicago, the Governor asked delegates to stay at the convention just one day longer. He told reporters that evening that he and his family would fly out first thing Saturday morning from Albany so the Governor could address the delegates in person in in Chicago Stadium to thank them for their nomination.

"I am going to leave at eight o'clock in the morning by airplane and expect to reach Chicago by about 2:30 our time," he told reporters Friday evening. It was no ordinary flight for the Governor, but he expressed a calm and a confidence as if it were. "I'm going to do some final work on the speech on the trip out," the Governor said, a speech that would be heard by millions of Americans across the country and the first to feature the Governor's promise of a New Deal for the country. He was eager to thank the delegates who'd selected him from a field that included at least two prominent rivals for his party's 1932 nomination. Former Governor Al Smith and Texas' Rep. John Nance Garner had both sought the nomination. Another five or so Democrats won a scattering of votes from delegates along with Smith and Garner, but Roosevelt's nomination in Chicago had never been especially close or in doubt. Roosevelt's selection was the culmination of the excitement that the Governor had built over months in Democratic primaries in some 16 states. His party's two-thirds nomination rule was still in place, so even as Roosevelt led as the clear front-runner with a majority of over 600 delegates on the first ballot, it had still taken three more ballots to reach two-thirds of the convention's more than 1,150 delegates.

"The speech tomorrow will be the notification so that we can save the expense," the Governor told reporters that Friday evening of his decision to accept his nomination in person at the Chicago Stadium, explaining that the break with tradition would spare the expense of holding an announcement speech weeks later in Albany. The flight also gave the Governor the opportunity to show the Democratic Party and the voters of the country that he intended to put everything he had and more into winning what was by no means a settled contest in November's campaign against President Herbert Hoover.

Saturday, July 2, 1932's flight from Albany, New York to Chicago was a moment like no other in an election year unlike any other in the twentieth century. *The New York Times'* James R. Kieran, Jr., a reporter traveling with the Governor and his family from Albany on their flight to Chicago, called it "the first utilization of the airplane in national politics," noting that the Ford Tri-Motor flew "through squalls and bumpy air" in heavy storms across the Great Lakes region that Saturday.[162] Along with *The New York Times'* Kieran and other reporters covering it, Roosevelt's flight and the coverage of the plane's arrival in Chicago was reported non-stop by the nation's radio networks, their broadcasts updating the flight's location throughout the day as Americans listened at home. Roosevelt's flight in the 13-seat Ford Tri-Motor that Saturday was the biggest story in the country. Hourly updates of the flight's progress captivated the country's imagination and held the attention of millions of radio listeners.

Governor Roosevelt and his family were met by a large and enthusiastic crowd of well-wishers on the tarmac of the Chicago Municipal Airport and then driven in a motorcade from the airport to Chicago Stadium. Over 1,100 delegates and thousands more in the audience awaited the Governor's arrival. Finally, Roosevelt entered Chicago Stadium and made his way to the podium in front of thousands of his fellow Democrats. Leaning into the bank of radio microphones in front of him on the podium, the Governor wrote a new chapter in the history of the Dem-

---

162 "Message Written on Way, Roosevelt Completed Text as the Plane Neared Toledo." *The New York Times* Sunday, July 3, 1932, 9.

ocrats and Republicans. That Saturday night in Chicago, Roosevelt changed forever the campaigning of America's presidential elections.

"My friends of the Democratic National Convention of 1932, I appreciate your willingness after these six arduous days to remain here, for I know well the sleepless hours which you and I have had," Roosevelt began shortly after 6:00 P.M., having been given a short introduction by Senator Thomas Walsh of Montana, the Chair of 1932's Democratic National Convention. "I regret that I am late, but I have had no control over the winds of Heaven and could only be thankful for my Navy training," the Governor joked of his flight from Albany. "The appearance before a national convention of its nominee for President before being formally notified of his selection is unprecedented and unusual, but these are unprecedented and unusual times," Roosevelt said. "I have started out on the many tasks that lie ahead by breaking the absurd tradition that the candidate should remain in professed ignorance of what has happened for weeks, until he is formally notified of that event many weeks later." "You have nominated me, and I know it, and I am here to thank you for the honor" the Governor told the Democratic delegates. "Let it be from now on the task of our party to break foolish traditions." "We will break foolish traditions and leave it to the Republican leadership to break promises," Roosevelt said as the crowd in Chicago Stadium applauded his words, and as those words carried far and wide to a country listening at homes to their radios.

"I pledge you, I pledge myself, to a New Deal for the American people," Roosevelt said in his speech to the Democratic National Convention and to the millions of American households listening on the radio in their homes on that Saturday evening. For the next 45 minutes, Roosevelt held forth on the failings of the Hoover White House and outlined his platform for expanding government's reach to restore the nation's shattered economy, finally finishing with the celebration and cheers of thousands to the Democratic anthem for the ages, "Happy Days are Here Again."[163] Democrats in Chicago Stadium and radio listeners across the United States saw and heard that evening the familiar, reassuring words they'd hear over the next decade, carrying them through the end of a Depression and the beginning of a World War.

Weeks earlier in Chicago Stadium on Tuesday, June 14, 1932, the Republican National Convention met in the same place to nominate President Herbert Hoover and Vice President Charles Curtis to the Republican ticket to run for a second term that fall. Unlike Roosevelt, Hoover did not fly or travel by train to Chicago to address the delegates, whose own convention, in the words of historian David Burner,

---

163 "Text of Governor Roosevelt's Speech at the Convention Accepting the Nomination." *The New York Times* Sunday, July 3, 1932, 8.

"[showed] a lack of enthusiasm for Hoover's renomination."[164] "No pictures of Hoover graced the convention hall," Burner tells us of the Republican convention. Weeks later from Washington, D.C. Hoover delivered his speech formally accepting his nomination for the fall 1932 ticket and thanking the delegates of the Republican National Convention weeks after they'd finished their work in Chicago. Hoover's acceptance speech on the evening of Thursday, August 11, 1932 to an audience of some 4,000 persons in Washington, D.C.'s Constitution Hall, a stately auditorium across the street from the White House, were broadcast by NBC and CBS and their affiliate stations to radio listeners across the country.[165] Hours earlier that Thursday afternoon, the President and his wife had invited some 500 visitors and well-wishers to the White House to thank them for their support before President Hoover's remarks that evening from Constitution Hall.

With a national economy still languishing from October 1929 when the bottom fell out, Roosevelt's selection by the Democrats and his historic flight from Albany to Chicago were the culmination of a series of consequential and fateful events for Roosevelt and his Democratic Party. Roosevelt's election as Governor in 1928, was one of the few bright spots nationally for Democrats, and the defeat of Al Smith by Commerce Secretary Herbert Hoover was one of the most disappointing but important defeats for Democrats nationally. Had Smith won the White House in 1928, the collapse of the nation's economy plunging the nation into Depression in less than a year's time easily might have been laid at the feet of the Democrats and Smith. Instead, Hoover's name became literally synonymous with the hardships of millions of desperate, destitute Americans, in the Hooverville shacks and shantytowns of evicted and unemployed Americans that sprang up everywhere in cities and towns across the country.

Everywhere Gov. Franklin Roosevelt and President Herbert Hoover spoke that fall of 1932, the appearance of radio microphones on the podiums in front of them as they spoke to audiences became a symbol of that fall's campaign in 1932. Millions of Americans stayed at home around their radios, some together with their families in their living rooms, others alone in the quiet of their bedrooms or kitchens, still others listening from outside through open windows to the radios of their neighbors, all leaning in and listening to the candidates in their speeches as they traveled and spoke with audiences and crowds across the United States. Micro-

---

164 David Burner, *Herbert Hoover: A Public Life.* Alfred A. Knopf, 1979, 307–308.
165 "Hoover Admits Failure of Prohibition, Declaring for State Control of Liquor, Would Barter War Debts in Trade Deal, Throng Sees Notification, President Goes Beyond His Platform by Urging Dry Law Change, Against Saloon's Return, Federal Check Demanded to Protect Dry States, Democratic Stand Attacked, Ban on Debt Cancellation, Panic Repelled, He Says, Resting Claim for Reelection on Economic Measures." *The New York Times* Friday, August 12, 1932, 1.

phone stands before the candidates often bore the network letters of CBS, NBC, or sometimes the station call-letters or even local station frequency-numbers of the local stations broadcasting the candidates and their words to listeners at home.

Millions of Americans saw and heard in person Hoover and Roosevelt and their campaigns by train as they crisscrossed the country that fall of 1932. For Roosevelt and his family, their train became almost a home-away-from-home for the better part of several months that fall. The rear-platform of the Governor's train featured a large placard reading "The Roosevelt Special" affixed to its rear-railing. As the Governor's train crisscrossed the country and stopped for trackside crowds, the rear-platform of the train would fill at each stop with Democratic elected officials and local candidates eager to be photographed with Roosevelt at his stops in their cities and towns. Much like sitting Presidents had done since President William Howard Taft's reelection bid in November 1912, President Hoover ran for reelection in the fall of 1932 with a mix of events at the White House and travels by the President by train across the country to speak with voters from the rear-platform of his own train, appearing in cities and towns together with fellow Republican candidates, hoping to build support for his ticket.[166]

Franklin Roosevelt's Tuesday, November 8, 1932 election saw historic victories for the Democrats across the board at the national level, including sweeping wins by Democratic candidates for the House and the Senate that built on the seats already won by the Democrats in 1930's midterms. Millions of Americans, including a 21-year old Ronald Reagan casting his first vote as a young man in Dixon, Illinois for the Governor, delivered the White House to the Democrats in 1932 and firmed up Democratic gains from November 1930's midterms in the House of Representatives and the Senate. President Hoover became the seventh sitting President to lose reelection to the White House, and the second sitting President to lose in the twentieth century.

"This great nation will endure as it has endured, will revive and will prosper," President Franklin D. Roosevelt said from the East Portico of the United State Capitol some weeks later to an audience estimated to be some 150,000 persons. Standing in front of the Capitol with the steps to the House and the Senate to either side, the President was sworn in at noon on Saturday, March 4, 1933, the last time an Inauguration would be held on the Constitutionally prescribed date of March fourth with the change of Inauguration Day to January twentieth coming under the Twentieth Amendment. "First of all, let me assert my firm belief that the

---

166 "Hoover Speeds West to Open Campaign, Gives Fighting Speech Tonight at Des Moines, Hopes He can Hold G.O.P. Farm Vote." *The Chicago Daily Tribune* Tuesday, October 4, 1932, 1.

only thing we have to fear is fear itself, nameless, unreasoning, unjustified terror which paralyzes needed efforts to convert retreat into advance," Roosevelt told the nation in one of the opening-lines of the 20-minute long address that Saturday on the steps of the Capitol.[167]

President Roosevelt wasted little time in the first days of his administration, immediately convening of an emergency session of Congress on Thursday, March 9, 1933, delivering his historic first Fireside Chat from the White House on Sunday evening, March 12, 1933, and inviting members of the White House press corps to crowd around the President's desk for the first time for his twice-weekly conferences with reporters in the West Wing.[168] Weeks into the Roosevelt White House, the beginnings of the New Deal took form in the frenetic pace of the seventy-third Congress with its Democratic House and Senate majorities.[169] The Tennessee Valley Authority (TVA), the Civilian Conservation Corps (CCC), and Banking Act of June 1933 all marked the beginnings of a more visible presence of the federal government in the lives of Americans in the first few months of the Roosevelt administration. Newly-created agencies like the Securities and Exchange Commission (SEC) built the foundations for a twentieth century of financial regulations after the Depression. So, too, the passage in the House and the Senate of the Twenty-First Amendment in February 1933, repealing the Eighteenth Amendment and restoring the legal manufacture, purchase, and sales of alcohol brought welcome relief of a different kind.[170] Confidence in banks and other financial institutions slowly but steadily showed signs of return, as the creation of the Federal Deposit

---

167 "Text of the Inaugural Address, President for Vigorous Action, 'This is Pre-Eminently the Time to Speak the Truth,' He Says, in Demand that 'the Temple of our Civilization be Restored to the Ancient Truths.'" *The New York Times* Sunday, March 5, 1933, 1.
168 "Questions Fly at Roosevelt at First Press Conference, Written Procedure Eliminated by President and Correspondents Applaud at Close of Session Lasting 40 Minutes, Executive Frank and Cordial." *The Washington Post* Thursday, March 9, 1933, 3.
169 "The Democratic Party in the 1930s became the reluctant instrument of a revolution it did not plan and it did not produce. It is hard to imagine a party less prepared for its new responsibilities than the Democratic Party was at the time of Franklin Roosevelt's first Inaugural," E.E. Schattschneider tells us 1960's *The Semisovereign People: A Realist's View of Democracy in America.* It is hard to imagine a better line – "It is hard to imagine a party less prepared for its new responsibilities than the Democratic Party" – to sum up the anxiousness and nervousness on the Democratic side of the aisle in March 1933. E.E. Schattschneider, *The Semisovereign People: A Realist's View of Democracy in America.* Holt, Reinhart, and Winston, 1960, 86.
170 "House Votes Dry Law Repeal 289 – 121, States Begin Move for Ratification, Lehman Asks Quick New York Action, House has Frenzied Day, Drys Fight for Floor as Debate is Cut Short by Rules Suspension, Wets Gibe at Blanton, He is Booed as He Tells of Threats to Put Him 'on the Spot,' Garner's Gavel is Futile, Rush Copies to States, Printers at Work on Resolution, So 40 Legislatures Now in Session Can Act." *The New York Times* Tuesday, February 21, 1933, 1.

Insurance Corporation (FDIC) and similar regulatory agencies and commissions placed scrutiny on banks as well as insured the savings accounts, mortgages, and other financial investments and loans for thousands of small businesses across the United States.

Weeks earlier, on Monday, January 23, 1933, Missouri became the thirty-sixth state to ratify the Twentieth Amendment establishing the start of newly-elected Congresses on January third and setting January twentieth as the start of the President's term in the White House.[171] "This amendment strikes from the government the time shackles that were placed upon it in the days of the stage coach, the saddle bags, and the tallow candle, when it required weeks for a legislator in the Georgia backwoods to make his way to the capital," *The Chicago Daily Tribune* told its readers.[172] From the second Wednesday in February as the date for the lame-duck House of Representatives to cast its one vote per state for one of three candidates in the event of the selection of the President in that chamber, the Twentieth Amendment changed the date for the casting of ballots for the President in the House. If no candidate for President won the majority of Electoral votes, House selection of the President from one of three candidates would now take place at the end of January, weeks after the newly-elected Congress had been sworn-in and started its work. Gone were the days when new Presidents might be selected by the old House.

1934's midterms saw the Democrats enlarge their House and Senate majority from 1932, as the White House saw some nine new seats in the House of Representatives and nine new Senate seats to enlarge their legislative undertakings in the second half of President Roosevelt's first term. Thursday, January 3, 1935's opening of the seventy-fourth Congress marked a historic moment for the Roosevelt White House and for the Democrats, with the enactment of the New Deal's landmark legacy for elderly Americans.

"Social Security Bill is Signed, Gives Pensions to Aged, Jobless," *The New York Times*' Thursday, August 15, 1935 headlines told readers, a bill backed~ overwhelmingly by Democrats in the House and Senate, along with the aisle-crossing votes of some 81 House Republicans and 16 Senate Republicans as a part of the legacy of the

---

171 "Thirty-Nine States Ratify Amendment Ending 'Lame Duck' Terms, Missouri is thirty-sixth to Vote Change in the Constitution, Effective on October 15, Inaugurations on January 20, Georgia, Utah and Ohio Legislatures Act Too, Term of Roosevelt Cut, Closes a Ten-Year Fight, Senator Norris Hails Result as a Blow to the Rule of Political Machines." *The New York Times* Tuesday, January 24, 1933, 1.

172 "Amendment to End Lame Duck Rule Adopted, 36 States Approve new Law." *The Chicago Daily Tribune* Tuesday, January 24, 1933, 1.

first term of President Franklin Roosevelt's administration.[173] Expanding the size of government as well as extending its reach into the biweekly and monthly earnings of every working American and into the bookkeeping and the payroll taxes of every business in America, Social Security made Washington, D.C. and the White House an even more central part of the lives of Americans for generations to come.[174] It also made it the focal point of unsuccessful lawsuits challenging its Constitutionality and the central issue of 1936's election.

Tuesday, November 3, 1936's election is remembered to this day as one of the liveliest, most energetic Depression-era campaigns between Democrats and Republicans in the twentieth century. Nominated at the Republican National Convention in Cleveland on the evening of Thursday, June 11, 1936, Kansas' then-Governor Alfred M. Landon took the customary route of not attending his nominating convention in Ohio in person, and instead stayed for its duration at the Governor's Mansion in Topeka.[175] Meanwhile, Roosevelt made history as the first sitting President to attend and address in person his party's national nominating convention, this time traveling to Philadelphia and speaking before the Democratic National Convention after it nominated him to run in the fall of 1936 for a second term. Roosevelt spoke to a massive crowd in Philadelphia with an audience of an estimated 100,000, braving the elements in the soaking-rain and filling the stands as they waited for hours for their chance to hear the President in a stadium near Philadelphia's Municipal Auditorium.

As his second time addressing the delegates of the Democratic National Convention in person, President Roosevelt didn't disappoint. There, on the evening of Saturday, June 26, 1936, Roosevelt spoke to some 100,000 in attendance and the millions more listening at home on radio. Roosevelt spoke of the many relief and recovery programs under-way and others still in-the-works in the Democratic

---

173 "Social Security Bill is Signed, Gives Pensions to Aged, Jobless, Roosevelt Approves Measure Intended to Benefit 30,000,000 Persons when States Adopt Cooperating Laws, He Calls the Measure 'Cornerstone' of his Economic Program." *The New York Times* Thursday, August 15, 1935, 1.

174 "Of all the changes the New Deal wrought, none surpassed in importance the transformation of public attitudes toward the federal government. Diplomat George F. Kennan, who grew up in the Midwest, once recalled that before the Depression, 'when times were hard, as they often were, groans and lamentations went up to God, but never to Washington.' After 1933, as never before, people directed their pleas to Washington, and within Washington to the President, who was rapidly eclipsing in public esteem Congress and all other participants in the New Deal." Patrick J. Maney, *The Roosevelt Presence: A Biography of Franklin Delano Roosevelt*. Simon and Schuster, 1992, 69.

175 "Landon Keeps Vigil Alone in Victory Hour." *The Chicago Daily Tribune* Friday, June 12, 1936, 1.

Congress, and hinted, too, at some of the frustration with the U.S. Supreme Court for several of its decisions reversing some important New Deal initiatives.

"This generation has a rendezvous with destiny," Roosevelt exhorted his crowd at the Democratic National Convention in Philadelphia on Saturday evening, June 26, 1936, and as his words broadcast nationally to millions more listening at home. "Today, my friends, we have won against the most dangerous of our foes, fear," the President told his audience, reprising his historic "fear itself" from Saturday, March 4, 1933's Inaugural. The President denounced Republicans as "economic royalists" and praised "the soundness of democracy in the midst of dictatorships." "We are fighting to save a great and precious form of government for ourselves and for the world," Roosevelt told his crowd that Saturday evening in Philadelphia, finishing his remarks with a victory-lap drive around Lincoln Field's horse-shoe track waving to the crowd.[176] Not until July 1948 when President Harry S. Truman traveled from Washington, D.C. to Philadelphia would another sitting President address the delegates of a national nominating convention.

As President Franklin D. Roosevelt made history as the first sitting President to travel from the White House to address their party's national nominating convention, so too did Roosevelt watch as Democrats dismantled one of the most embarrassing anachronisms of the Democratic Party, namely the antiquity of the two-thirds nomination rule from the era of Jackson, Van Buren, and Douglas that was still in place despite the many calls to change or remove it over the years. Thursday, June 25, 1936's Democratic National Convention vote to end the nomination rule was largely done without much disagreement among most Democrats.[177] With 36 state delegations voting to end the nomination rule to just 13 delegations casting their votes in favor of keeping it, the century-old rule came to an uneventful end. With its history dating back over 100 years to May 1832's Democratic National Convention under President Andrew Jackson and Martin Van Buren, few Democratic leaders were disappointed to see two-thirds nomination rule go in the era of coast-to-coast network radio broadcasts.

---

176 "Salvos of Cheers Greet President, Serried Banks of Humanity on Field Hang on the Words of His Acceptance Speech, Applaud Mandate Call, Garner Ceremony Speeded to Bring Roosevelt Before Party as Standard-Bearer Again." *The New York Times* Sunday, June 28, 1936, 1, 25.

177 "Democrats Adopt Platform Continuing New Deal, Favor Constitutional Amendments, if Necessary, Convention Abrogates Century-Old Two-Thirds Rule, South Bows to Change, Appeased by Promise to Reapportion as Two-Thirds Rule Ends, Fight on Floor Avoided, Committee Instructs Party Heads to Work out New Representation Basis, On Democratic Vote Cast, Southerners Will be Relatively Stronger than Delegates of Less 'Regular' States." *The New York Times* Friday, June 26, 1936, 1.

In the fall of 1936, Governor Alf Landon and his running mate, Chicago's Frank Knox, publisher of *The Chicago Daily News,* mounted their bid to take the White House from President Roosevelt, taking any number of pages from the Democratic Party's playbook as Republicans waged an energetic campaign to unseat Roosevelt. Landon spent the early weeks of the race planning out the Republican campaign from the Kansas statehouse in Topeka, where Landon made frequent radio broadcasts on a host of different topics on the nation's coast-to-coast radio networks. By the early fall, Landon, with the distinctive Kansas sunflower as the symbol of his campaign in buttons, pins, posters, billboards, and bumper-stickers, set out to travel across the country by train to take the Republican Party's platform and promises to the American electorate.[178] In an era where Landon might easily have flown by airplane from city to city to cover much further distances in a shorter time, here was a Midwest Governor taking his message by train to the people in their own backyards and railyards. The Governor and his family and his staff traveled by train from city to city and town to town in the fall of 1936, bringing out some of the largest rail-yard audiences ever for any Republican candidate in the decades since President William Howard Taft in November 1912 took to the nation's railroads for the first time to travel and talk with the country's voters.

Traveling from the Kansas capitol across the country by train in the fall of 1936, Landon traveled thousands of miles and spoke to the large crowds that stood on either side of the railroad tracks around the rear-platform of Landon's train at each of its stops. From two large loudspeakers mounted atop the roof of the train's rear platform and visible in countless black-and-white photographs from the fall of 1936, Landon railed against the President and rallied Republicans from Topeka to Buffalo and back, finishing his first major trip that August with speeches in Chicago and in St. Louis and then across Missouri to Kansas City before returning to the Kansas capital. That fall, Landon made the most of the nation's railways and of the coast-to-coast radio networks to reach millions of Americans either in person or over the airwaves. Weeks of speaking to railyard crowds, shaking hands with voters, and logging thousands of miles by train finally ended for the Governor with his last speech of the fall campaign before some 16,000 supporters in downtown St. Louis, Missouri on Saturday, October 31, 1936, before returning to Topeka to await the country's returns that Tuesday.

In Tuesday, November 3, 1936's election, the Roosevelt White House won a resounding reelection with Democrats sweeping seats from coast-to-coast, the fourth election in a row where Democrats bested the Republicans. President Roosevelt

---

178 Ralph D. Casey, "Republican Propaganda in the 1936 Campaign." *The Public Opinion Quarterly* 1, no. 2, April 1937, 27–44.

carried 46 of 48 states for the President's reelection to a second term including his rival's home state ("Even Kansas Goes For the President," Wednesday, November 4, 1936's headlines told readers of *The New York Times*) as well as the Republican Vice-Presidential nominee Frank Knox's home state of Illinois in a reelection race that was never that close. Democrats came out of 1936's election with some 334 seats in the House of Representatives and 76 Democratic Senate seats, leaving a solid swath of Democratic House districts stretching across the Midwest and through the South and then stretching up into the Great Lakes and into the Northeast. In the heart of Texas' Hill Country, a 28-year old Lyndon Johnson was among the newly-elected Democrats winning seats in the House, carrying Texas' tenth Congressional District in a special election on Saturday, April 10, 1937 to fill the seat of the late Representative James P. "Buck" Buchanan.[179] White House successes slowed somewhat with the stumble over the President's ill-considered proposals to increase the size of the U.S. Supreme Court shortly after 1936's election, a stumble that, together with financial setbacks in the recovery from the Great Depression, set back the Democrats who kept their majority but saw losses in 1938's midterms.

"I intend to give everything I have," Wendell L. Willkie told Republican National Convention delegates that Thursday, June 27, 1940, in Philadelphia's Convention Hall, the first Republican presidential nominee to deliver remarks in person to delegates at their national nominating convention. A lifelong Democrat who appealed throughout the fall of 1940 to Democrats disillusioned with the Roosevelt White House and the President's decision to seek an unprecedented third term, Willkie as the nominee of the Republican ticket for 1940's election brought a unique if at times unconventional energy and enthusiasm to his campaign.[180] While Roosevelt spent most of the fall of 1940's campaign at home in the White House and did not attend July 1940's Democratic National Convention as he had in 1932 and 1936, Willkie spoke in person to Republicans in Philadelphia. Willkie traveled some 30,000 miles that fall by airplane, automobile, and train, with millions of Americans crowding to his rallies curious to see a Republican campaign that at times ap-

---

179 "Texan Backing Court Plan Wins Congress Seat." *The Chicago Daily Tribune* Sunday, April 11, 1937, 8.
180 "Some 2,000,000 people flocked to hear him, many, perhaps out of curiosity – as he revealed *political views which often resembled those of the New Deal.* But here it was the end of September [1940], and the Republican challenger had failed to campaign in the East. 'What does?' asked disgruntled and worried Eastern leaders. 'Why is he wasting his time in the West?' It was difficult for these men to understand why Willkie insisted on making a major address in Arizona where only three Electoral votes were at stake." Henry O. Evjen, "The Willkie Campaign: An Unfortunate Chapter in Republican Leadership." *The Journal of Politics* 14, no. 2, May 1952, 250, Italics added.

peared to endorse parts of the New Deal platform.[181] Billboards, bumper stickers, buttons, and boundless other knickknacks and merchandise featured the frowning image of Uncle Sam in red, white, and blue turning his thumb downwards and the words "No third term," sometimes also including the line Democrats for Willkie, while Democrats including Al Smith and James A. Farley backed Willkie in November 1940.

When all was said and done, and much was said in the thousands of "I'm a Willkie Democrat" and "Democrats for Willkie" banners, billboards, buttons, and bumper-stickers, the historic third-term reelection of President Franklin Roosevelt was never a close contest. Willkie won just 82 Electoral votes in Tuesday, November 5, 1940's election, carrying only Illinois and Michigan as the Republican's largest states that election night. Democratic majorities held in the House and the Senate, majorities that would cast the historic Monday, December 8, 1941 votes declaring war on Japan. Wartime's changes to the lives of every American included a rising generation of soon-to-be-elected figures like Lieutenant John F. Kennedy, Lieutenant Commander Richard M. Nixon, Major General and Supreme Commander Allied Expeditionary Forces Dwight D. Eisenhower, First Lieutenant George McGovern, Lieutenant George H.W. Bush, Second Lieutenant Robert J. Dole, and others.

Days before July 1944's Democratic National Convention in the Chicago Stadium, President Franklin Roosevelt told White House reporters he would be willing to accept the party's nomination for a fourth term. "Reluctantly, but as a good soldier," the President told reporters in the White House at the end of one of his press conferences with reporters on Tuesday, July 11, 1944, "I will accept and serve in this office, if I am so ordered by the Commander in Chief of us all, the sovereign people of the United States." For weeks, Roosevelt sidestepped questions by reporters about his interest in running for a fourth term, but now with just days to go before the Chicago convention, he expressed his willingness to accept nomination by his party.[182] Roosevelt did not attend the Democratic National Convention in person,

---

181 Willkie's support for unemployment relief, for Social Security and for the recently enacted federal hourly minimum wage seemingly underscored the extent to which the Roosevelt White House had pushed the Republicans to what some in Willkie's party complained was a "me too" Republicanism, a sentiment familiar in its recurrence in the years to come in the criticism of Thomas Dewey by some of his fellow Republicans. "G.O.P. Elephant Taken for Ride by New Dealers," *The Chicago Daily Tribune*'s headlines said on Wednesday, June 23, 1948 during the party's Philadelphia parlay. "'Me-Too' Boys are High in the Howdah," *The Chicago Daily Tribune* headlines harrumphed. "G.O.P. Elephant Taken for Ride by New Dealers, 'Me-Too' Boys are High in the Howdah." *The Chicago Daily Tribune* Wednesday, July 23, 1948, 5.
182 "F.D.R. to Run, He Reveals it with a Flourish, Seeks a Fourth Term 'Reluctantly.'" *The Chicago Daily Tribune* Wednesday, July 12, 1944, 1.

but his train stopped in Chicago for meetings with party leaders days before hundreds of Democratic delegates arrived in the city. Roosevelt was en route to San Diego, where just days later, the President began an inspection tour in the Pacific and met with General Douglas MacArthur. Days later, Roosevelt accepted his nomination and thanked the Democratic National Convention in a broadcast from his train ("President Says Yes from Train on West Coast," *The Chicago Daily Tribune*'s front-page headlines said on Friday, July 21, 1944) as he prepared for his travels in the Pacific.[183] In that moment, Democratic Senator Harry S. Truman of Missouri took one step closer to his own moment in history as he emerged from closed-door sessions by party heavyweights as their choice for Roosevelt's running-mate for his fourth term bid.

Tuesday, November 7, 1944's wartime election was in some respects America's Democrats and Republicans at their best, as President Franklin D. Roosevelt and then-Governor Thomas E. Dewey sought to energize their own ranks yet both kept their campaigns focused as always on the unification of the country in wartime's fight. Losing even his home state of New York, then-Governor Dewey's states were mostly won in the Central Plains and in the Great Lakes. With the death of President Roosevelt in April 1945, new and unprecedented challenges awaited the Democrats and Republicans after the war's end, most powerfully of which were the first stirrings of a powerful postwar movement for civil rights and racial equality. The arrival of commercial television in the postwar moment, the construction of the first stretches of the federally-financed interstate highways, the growth in air conditioning and other appliances and conveniences in the home, even the rise of postwar room-sized mainframe computers, all of these changes marked the end of the wartime moment, and all anticipated the far-reaching changes in the lives of Americans in the years after the war.

Tuesday, November 5, 1946's midterms were the first postwar election for the United States, midterms that marked a short-shift to Republicans in the House and in the Senate. House and Senate majorities for the Republicans, the so-called do-nothing Congress made famous just two years later by President Truman, brought a new generation of elected officials to the national stage in January 1947. Lieutenant John F. Kennedy and Lieutenant Commander Richard M. Nixon were among a rising postwar generation elected in Tuesday, November 5, 1946's midterms, Kennedy in Massachusetts' eleventh District in Boston and Nixon in California's twelfth District in Southern California's Pasadena and Pomona.

Tuesday, November 2, 1948's election is the last presidential election before the arrival of commercial television broadcasting, the last election before the begin-

---

183 "President Says Yes from Train on West Coast." *The Chicago Daily Tribune* Friday, July 21, 1944, 1.

ning of more affordable commercial air travel, and the last election just before the first construction of stretches of the federal interstate highway that changed the lives of every American. In every way, 1948's election was the first of the postwar America changed campaigns for Democrats and Republicans. Commercial television kept more Americans indoors as did the arrival of postwar appliances, like dishwashers and washing machines as well as air-conditioning. Airlines took the campaigns of postwar presidential elections out of the railyards and took them to the tarmacs of airports. All changed the way that Democrats and Republicans worked to reach voters in postwar America.

June 1948's Republican National Convention meeting in Philadelphia's Municipal Auditorium is the last national nominating convention for the Republicans to have had its delegates cast more than just a first ballot for the state-by-state tally for its presidential nomination, the measure of commercial broadcast television's arrival as a force for the Democrats and Republicans favoring fewer late-night, multi-ballot brawls for the nomination. With six leading candidates in the Republican field, it took three ballots for Republican National Convention delegates to select the party's nominee, New York's then-Governor Thomas E. Dewey.[184] In yet another measure of the changing part of the national nominating conventions in the era of nationally televised broadcasting, all six of the leading Republican presidential candidates hoping to be on the fall 1948 ticket were all in Philadelphia, most of them accompanied by their wives and by their families featured in radio and television interviews, newspaper stories, and black-and-white photographs for newspapers and weekly newsmagazines.[185] Former Governor Harold Stassen, Representative Joseph Martin of Massachusetts, Governor Thomas E. Dewey, Senator Robert A. Taft of Ohio, Governor Earl Warren of California, and Senator Edward Martin of Pennsylvania all traveled to Philadelphia, all met with delegates, all spoke with the press, and each addressed the delegates and the radio listeners and television viewers watching the convention at home. Never before in the history of either the Democratic or the Republican conventions had so many candidates seeking their party's nomination been present in person at a national nominating convention to make the case for their nomination, as each of the six potential nominees in Philadelphia were prepared to accept their nomination in person and to speak before the delegates and before the nation in their televised

---

184 "Dewey Unanimous Republican Choice for President on the Third Ballot, Running Mate Will be Named Today, Opposition Falls, Taft and Stassen Join in Urging Selection of New Yorker, G.O.P. Precedent Set, Dewey is First Defeated Candidate to be Chosen Again." *The New York Times* Friday, June 25, 1948, 1.
185 "At the Opening Sessions of the Twenty-Fourth Republican National Convention in Philadelphia Yesterday." *The New York Times* Tuesday, June 22, 1948, 3.

remarks, a moment with little precedent in the history of the national nominating conventions.

Having delivered his own speech to the Democratic National Convention also meeting in Philadelphia's Municipal Auditorium in the early-morning hours of Thursday, July 15, 1948, President Harry S. Truman became the second sitting President in history to address his party's nominating convention. Yet, Truman's acceptance speech delivered at almost two o'clock in the morning to exhausted delegates and the few television viewers at home still awake in the cities with television broadcasting had been delayed by a walk-out of all 22 delegates from Mississippi's delegation as well as 13 members of the Alabama delegation. Convening their own nominating convention just three days later in Birmingham, Alabama, the States' Rights Democratic Party and its splinter fall ticket of then-Governor J. Strom Thurmond of South Carolina and then-Governor Fielding Wright of Mississippi might well either divided Democrats nationally enough to ease the election of the Republican ticket or led to an election in the U.S. House of Representatives for the third time in the nation's history. Still, President Truman's razor-edge re-election on Tuesday, November 2, 1948, was a remarkable moment not least of which is well-remembered in the iconic *The Chicago Daily Tribune* headline.

"Dewey Defeats Truman," *The Chicago Daily Tribune*'s Tuesday, November 2, 1948 headline is one of the enduring and indelible images of postwar American politics. "Dewey Defeats Truman" had been one of several headlines printed by *The Chicago Daily Tribune* early in the evening on Tuesday, November 2, 1948, as its editors rushed to get the latest news out to the sidewalks and to the newsstands of Chicago. "Governor Dewey Claims Victory," *The Chicago Daily Tribune*'s headlines of another, less famous edition that evening mistakenly told that paper's readers. By the third or fourth of what are believed to have been at least ten or eleven different editions printed by *The Chicago Daily Tribune* that evening and into the early-morning Wednesday hours, editors had corrected their earlier misprint. "Early Dewey Lead Narrows," front-page headlines closer to midnight now told the late-night readers of *The Chicago Daily Tribune* as uncertainly over the election-returns in California, Ohio, and elsewhere kept millions of radio listeners awake late that Tuesday evening for the latest breaking reports and updates. Finally, by the early-morning hours that Wednesday, election returns confirmed the results. Truman had won his second term in the White House. Narrow victories in California, Illinois and Ohio proved decisive as the final-returns were reported. Democrats also took back the House and the Senate from the Republicans. Word of the President's reelection arrived to him at his campaign's headquarters on the seventeenth floor of Kansas City's Muehlebach Hotel that Wednesday morning, and it was on President Truman's trip the following day from Missouri back to the nation's capital that his train stopped at St. Louis' Union Station where he was handed and held aloft the historic copy of *The Chicago Daily Tribune*'s "Dewey Defeats Truman" edition.

In one of the most storied bids of the twentieth century for reelection to the White House, President Harry S. Truman won a bruising campaign on Tuesday, November 2, 1948, an election whose indelible memories decades later is not just in *The Chicago Daily Tribune*'s headline but also in its black-and-white photographs of both the President and his Republican rival taking to the nation's railways in the last great battle of the railroads between the Democrats and the Republicans. 1948's election was a railyards battle for every vote where the President of the United States and the Governor of the largest state in the United States stopped their trains to speak to voters in towns that were so small that the trains didn't normally stop there unless passengers were seen up ahead at the side of the tracks by engineers. Truman and Dewey stopping their trains to talk with voters and to talk with newspaper reporters crowded on their trains as they traveled across the miles from city to city and town to town made 1948 a year like no other in the twentieth century in a moment when elections and the campaigning of candidates were about to change forever in the era of airlines and television.

With America's postwar television viewers paying attention and watching like never before beginning in the early 1950s, national nominating conventions for Democrats and Republicans shed their past of back-room bargains and late-night brawls that selected candidates in days of balloting and battling, and turned them into well-scripted, planned-to-the-minute TV broadcast-productions for Democratic and Republican candidates already determined by the patchwork of state-by-state presidential primaries and caucuses. With the arrival of postwar commercial television broadcasting and the coast-to-coast network broadcasts of the early 1950s, delivering the right impression to millions of television viewers at home became the singular focus of the national nominating conventions. A new generation of Democratic and Republican staff and strategists now gave attention like never to the scripting of the speeches by the presidential candidates and every other part of the nationally-televised nominating conventions.

1952's election of President-elect Dwight D. Eisenhower and his Vice-Presidential running-mate Richard M. Nixon shifted the tectonic-plates of the Democrats and the Republicans for the next decade, a decade defined by the split-screen of a Republican White House and Democratic House and Senate majorities throughout most of the 1950s. It was an election of change, the continued growth of commercial television broadcasting and the arrival of the nation's coast-to-coast TV networks, the continued growth of state-by-state presidential primary elections, and the growing calls for nationally-televised debates between the Democratic and Republican candidates in their fall contests, something that had never happened in all the years of commercial radio broadcasting.[186] Dwight Eisenhower's 1952 election returned the Republicans for a short-lived, two-year stint in the House and Senate majority, a majority lost for the Eisenhower White House in the next midterm in 1954 and not won again by the Republicans in the House for another 40 years.

"Democrats Control House by 27, Apparently Will Rule Senate, President Pledges Cooperation," Thursday, November 4, 1954's *The New York Times*' headlines told of the latest turn in the back-and-forth between Democrats and Republicans in 1954's midterms, gains this time by Democrats that they did not lose to the Republicans for another four decades in the House. [187] 1954's midterm losses for the Republicans in the House and the Senate mark in many respects a prelude for the next generation, one with Democratic-led Congresses and with the back-and-forth Democratic and Republican White House administrations in an era of political protests, social upheaval, and international conflict. 1956's reelection of President Dwight Eisenhower and Vice President Richard M. Nixon, a split-screen election with the reelection of a Republican White House and the reelection of Democratic-led House and Senate chambers.

"Stevenson Is Nominated on the Third Ballot, Pledges Fight 'With All My Heart and Soul,' Truman Promises to 'Take Off Coat' and Help, Rivals Drop Out, Withdrawal of Harriman Starts States' Rush to the Governor, Illinoisan Trailed, But Picked Up Strength from Larger States," *The New York Times*' front-page headlines told readers of Saturday, July 26, 1952's nomination of Adlai Stevenson on the third ballot at the Democratic National Convention, a history-making headline as the last contested convention for either the Democrats or Republicans with its three state-by-state roll-call votes on the floor of the Chicago Amphitheater after Tennessee's then-Senator Estes Kefauver, Georgia's then-Senator Richard B. Russell, Jr., and others fell short on the first and second ballots and Gov. Adlai Stevenson was selected on the third and last contested ballot in the history of the national nominating con-

---

186 For the second election in a row, the Democratic National Convention and the Republican National Convention – both in July 1952 – are hosted in the same city, Chicago, Illinois, and the same amphitheater, the International Amphitheater on the city's Southside at 4220 South Halsted St., equipped that year with costly network TV equipment for the coast-to-coast broadcasts. That summer, a new air conditioning system had been installed so that the nation's Democrats and Republicans were more comfortable in the heat of the bright lights used by network technicians during the broadcasts.

187 Republican losses left the Democrats that Tuesday, November 2, 1954 with a 48–47 Senate majority and with 232–203 in the House – majorities for the Democrats in November 1954's midterms that they held for the better part of a generation. Kenneth C. Martis, *The Historical Atlas of the Political Parties in the United States Congress, 1789–1989*. Macmillan Publishing Company, 1989, 209.

ventions. Thursday, August 16, 1956's nomination of Stevenson on the first ballot at the Democratic National Convention is the end of the brawling, drawn-out, multi-ballot nominations for the Democrats.

With Stevenson's nomination on the first ballot at Chicago's International Amphitheatre on Thursday, August 16, 1956 and President Dwight D. Eisenhower's nod on the first ballot on Wednesday, August 22, 1956 at San Francisco's legendary Cow Palace, Democrats and Republicans in every convention since have chosen their presidential tickets on the first ballot, as the shifting of the nomination fights away from the floors of the national nominating conventions to the state-by-state caucuses, conventions, and primaries in the postwar era coincided with coast-to-coast television broadcasting's watchful eye at the nominating conventions marked the end of contested conventions. TV transformed the national party conventions, and it was about to transform the Fall campaigns in even more far-reaching ways with the first nationally televised presidential debates.

"Good evening," CBS' Howard K. Smith told over 70,000,000 Americans in words that forever changed campaigning and elections of the President of the United States. "The television and radio stations of the United States and their affiliated stations are proud to provide facilities for a discussion of issues in the current political campaign by the two major candidate for the Presidency," CBS' Smith said to an audience of over 70,000,000 Americans on Monday, September 26, 1960, watching history in the making from Chicago's WBBM-TV Channel 2 studios. That Monday evening, then-Senator John F. Kennedy of Massachusetts and then-Vice President Richard M. Nixon faced off in downtown Chicago from the studios of WBBM-TV in the first of four live nationally televised debates.

"The Columbia Broadcasting System has put a fresh coat of paint on the interior of its studio at 630 McClurg Ct. where a small army of technicians, newsmen, photographers, police, and politicians will gather while the principals talk," *The Chicago Tribune* reported on Sunday, September 25, 1960, and carried on each of the nation's three television networks.[188] Over the next month, Kennedy and Nixon faced off in three more live, nationally televised debates, each drawing tens of millions of viewers. In all of the years of commercial radio broadcasting, no presidential debates had ever aired between Democrats and Republicans. Now, only a few years into the era of commercial TV broadcasting, nationally televised presidential debates debuted. Months of televised appearances, debates, and interviews preceded the historic debates between Democratic and Republican candidates together on the stages of TV studios in Chicago, Washington, D.C., Los An-

---

188 "Stage Set for Kennedy, Nixon on CBS, Rivals to be Cool, Undistracted." *The Chicago Tribune* Sunday, September 25, 1960, 1.

geles (where Nixon appeared in the studios of KABC-TV in a coast-to-coast split-screen televised debate against Kennedy, who was in an ABC studio on New York City's West Sixty-Sixth Street), and New York City in the first nationally televised debates and related TV coverage like no other presidential contest to date.

Tuesday, November 8, 1960's election saw President-elect John Kennedy win a historic, razor-thin victory over then-Vice President Nixon, having both started their rise to national office together in 1946's midterms and then fighting to a photo-finish nationally in Tuesday, November 8, 1960's race. In California and elsewhere, returns were so close that it took days to tally the final vote, and determine that Vice President Nixon had narrowly carried his home state of California and its 32 Electoral votes. 1960's election is still remembered to this day as one of the closest races in the twentieth century, a year unlike any other when it is impossible to not conclude that the historic four nationally televised debates affected the hair's-breadth margins in some of those photo-finish states.

"Bomb Blast Kills Four Children, Injures 17 at Church Here," *The Birmingham Post-Herald*'s Monday, September 16, 1963 morning headlines said to a shattered nation. "Kennedy Slain on Dallas Street, Johnson Becomes President," *The Dallas Morning News*' headlines of Saturday morning, November 23, 1963 told a mourning nation. Violence shattering the optimism of the nation in the shooting of President Kennedy, violence strengthening the resolve of the civil rights movement and the struggles of Americans in all parts of the country to fulfill the promise of nonviolence even in the face of such tragedies in the death of President Kennedy in Dallas and the deaths of Carol Denise McNair, Carole Robertson, Addie Mae Collins, and Cynthia Wesley, along with the murders of James Earl Chaney, Andrew Goodman, and Michael Henry Schwerner in Mississippi's Neshoba County months later on the evening of Sunday, June 21, 1965. Churches bombed. Churches burned. Escalating war in Southeast Asia and the boiling and roiling anger everywhere from its most elite college campuses to the most impoverished neighborhoods and tenement buildings in the country lit the fires of leaders like President Lyndon Johnson, the Reverend Dr. Martin Luther King, Jr. and so many others to hold the country together through some of the most important and sweeping legislative victories in the country's history for protecting the lives of America's elderly as well as the pursuing the promise of full citizenship for millions of African-Americans.

"I will offer a choice not an echo," Republican Senator Barry Goldwater said, in his campaign announcement speech on the patio of his home in Paradise City, a suburb of Phoenix, Arizona on Friday, January 3, 1964, setting the stage for the convulsions that cut across and cut through the Democrats and Republicans in the next year's election and in the decades to come.[189] Sen. Goldwater welcomed Democrats in the South that summer and fall defecting from Democratic President Lyndon B. Johnson in droves, offset by millions of Republicans put off by their nominee. Tuesday, November 3, 1964's election saw the reelection of President Lyndon B. Johnson as then-Sen. Goldwater's fall ticket left the nation so divided that some of President Johnson's states including Kansas, North Dakota, and South Dakota, states that hadn't cast their vote for a Democratic national ticket since 1936's reelection of President Franklin D. Roosevelt and wouldn't cast votes again for the Democratic national ticket. Washington, D.C. voters cast their first votes for President under the Twenty-Third Amendment.[190] Tuesday, November 3, 1964's elections saw Democrats win 295–140 seats in the House and carry a 68–32 Democratic Senate majority in the eighty-ninth Congress, majorities that saw enactment of the landmark legacies of the Johnson White House of July 1965's Medicare and August 1965's Voting Rights Act.

"I think New Hampshire is the only place where a candidate can claim 20% is a landslide and 40% is a mandate and 60% is unanimous," President Lyndon B. Johnson joked in a speech to the Veterans of Foreign Wars in Washington, D.C. the evening of Tuesday, March 12, 1968.[191] It was just hours after final-returns of New Hampshire's Democratic presidential primary ballots, where Minnesota Democratic Senator Eugene McCarthy made headlines with the help of hundreds of young volunteers winning some 42% of New Hampshire's Democratic vote in a party-splitting primary bid against his own party's Democratic President Lyndon B. Johnson, the first time for a major challenge in the primaries since 1912. Four days later on Saturday, March 16, 1968, New York Democratic Senator Robert F. Kennedy entered the Democratic primary race.[192] "I do not run for the Presidency merely to oppose any man but to propose new policies," Senator Kennedy told the nation in his speech entering the race against Johnson.

"I shall not seek, and I will not accept, the nomination of my party for another term as your President," Johnson finally told viewers watching a nationally televised broadcast from the White House on the evening of Sunday, March 31, 1968. In the closing-moments of a nationally televised broadcast from the Oval Office,

189 "Goldwater Says He'll Run to Give Nation a 'Choice,' He Joins G.O.P. Presidential Race with Vow to Hew to His Conservatism, Sees a Hard Contest, Arizonan Planning to Enter New Hampshire Primary, He Chides Johnson." *The New York Times* Saturday, January 4, 1964, 1.
190 "Big Capital Vote Goes to Johnson, Goldwater Fails to Carry a Single Precinct in City." *The New York Times* Wednesday, November 4, 1964, 3.
191 "Lyndon Pokes Fun at First Primary Vote." *The Chicago Tribune* Wednesday, March 13, 1968, 6.
192 "Kennedy to Make Three Primary Races, Attacks Johnson, Challenge Issued, Senators Says only New Leaders can Change Divisive Policies." *The New York Times* Sunday, March 17, 1968, 1.

President Johnson stunned viewers and surprised most of his staff outside of a handful of his closest advisors, aides, and family that he wouldn't run for a second term, nor would he accept renomination by the Democratic National Convention, scheduled to meet in Chicago's International Amphitheatre on the city's Southside in August. Days later, the assassination of the Reverend Dr. Martin Luther King, Jr. on the balcony of the Lorraine Motel in Memphis, Tennessee on Thursday, April 4, 1968, sparked riots and violence for a country already tearing itself apart. The assassination of Senator Robert F. Kennedy of New York on the evening of Tuesday, June 4, 1968, at Los Angeles' Ambassador Hotel celebrating his just-announced victory in California's Democratic presidential primary only sparked still more disillusionment and discontent, compounded by the protests and violence in the streets of Chicago at the end of August 1968 at the Democratic National Convention.

Tuesday, November 5, 1968's election of President-elect Richard M. Nixon was far closer and much more hard-fought than Tuesday, November 7, 1972's reelection of President Nixon. Where 1972 saw a 49-state defeat of then-Senator George McGovern of South Dakota, 1968 was an extraordinarily close election, complicated by the candidacy of former Alabama Governor George Wallace. Split-the-difference elections of Democratic House and Senate majorities in 1968 tamped back and tempered Nixon's victory celebrations. Throughout the evening of 1968's vote, President-elect Richard M. Nixon asked aides repeatedly after his own election was certain what returns were looking like for House and Senate races still being tabulated late into the evening, a tabulation that when finally tallied that night kept the Democrats in the majority in the House and in the Senate, and that kept President-elect Nixon from being elected with his own party in charge of either chamber, something that hadn't happened since Whig President Zachary Taylor's election in 1848.[193]

"Five Held in Plot to Bug Democrats' Office Here," *The Washington Post*'s Sunday, June 18, 1972 headlines reported in a story bylined that morning by *The Washington Post*'s Alfred E. Lewis, an investigation and reporting taken over the next morning in Monday, June 19, 1972's *The Washington Post* by reporters Bob Woodward and Carl Bernstein with their "G.O.P. Security Aide Among Five Arrested in Bugging Affair" as the first of scores of stories and reports bylined by the *Post* reporters. The historic arrests at offices at the Democratic National Committee (DNC)

---

193 "It was the first presidential election since Zachary Taylor's in 1848 that left the opposition in control of the House and Senate. [President-elect Richard M.] Nixon's own mood ought to have been very good. Lee Huebner, who was about to join Nixon's staff as a speechwriter, remembers making his way into the Waldorf and congratulating the President-elect. 'And he shook his head and said, "No, no, we lost both houses of the Congress."'" Jeffrey Frank, *Ike and Dick: Portrait of a Strange Political Marriage*. Simon and Schuster 2013, 316.

on the sixth floor of the Watergate Office Building at 2:30 A.M. on Saturday, June 17, 1972 was actually the 2nd break in, following a Saturday, March 27, 1972 break-in when burglars had first broken in to the DNC offices and eluded arrest. Monday morning, June 19, 1972's Bob Woodward and Carl Bernstein "G.O.P. Security Aide Among Five Arrested in Bugging Affair" byline in *The Washington Post* marked the start of one of the most historic chapters in the twentieth century for Democrats and Republicans.

Tuesday, November 7, 1972's 49-state, 520 Electoral vote-sweep in the reelection of President Richard M. Nixon was a split-decision just like 1968. 1972's election of a 242 – 192 House Democratic majority and a 56 – 44 Senate Democratic majority the same night as the President's 49-state reelection were the Democratic and Republican members of the ninety-third Congress who would take part in the Senate Select Committee on Presidential Campaign Activities and in the House Judiciary Committee's impeachment proceedings. Thursday, May 17, 1973's start of nationally televised hearings by the Senate Select Committee on Presidential Campaign Activities and then the television broadcasts of the House Judiciary Committee starting on the evening of Wednesday, July 24, 1974 brought TV into the chambers, hallways, and meeting rooms of Capitol Hill for the first time. They also brought the investigation and work of Capitol Hill into the living rooms of homes of an estimated 90,000,000 Americans who watched some part of the long months of hearings, investigations, revelations, and witnesses culminating in the Friday, August 9, 1974 resignation and departure from the White House with a wave from the steps of Marine One by President Richard M. Nixon as he left office and left the Republican Party reeling.

In Tuesday, November 5, 1974's midterms, Democrats built their House and Senate majorities in the worst of the Watergate moment, weeks after President Richard M. Nixon waved boarding Marine One, and weeks after President Gerald R. Ford's controversial pardon of President Nixon on Sunday morning, September 8, 1974. It was a time of testing for the Constitution and of the Democrats and Republicans few Americans living through it would ever forget. For the Republicans, it was a moment where the name if not the very existence of the Republican Party after 120-years of history was seen as in doubt by some of its leading lawmakers, figures like Ronald Reagan, Newt Gingrich, and others who considered renaming the Republicans or even starting an entirely new party.[194] For the Demo-

---

194 "Some Republicans Fearful Party Is on Its Last Legs." *The New York Times* Monday, May 31, 1976, 1, 16. "I want to enlist support among the growing numbers of independents and disappointed Democrats for a new Republican Party," Ronald Reagan told a gathering of Republicans at their low-water moment. Speaking to a gathering of Republican leaders in Boston on Friday, November 19, November 1976, just days after President-elect Carter's victory, Reagan expressed his own dis-

crats, it was a moment where the party of Jackson, Cleveland, Wilson, and Roose-velt stood again squarely in the spotlight of history, the reaffirmation of the resil-iency of both parties, shown in the bipartisan aisle-crossing in the House Judiciary Committee's votes on articles of impeachment with Republican Judiciary Commit-tee members voting for the impeachment articles and in then-Sen. Barry Goldwa-ter and other Senate Republicans breaking the news to Nixon in a White House meeting on Wednesday, August 7, 1974 that there weren't enough Republican Sen-ators to keep Nixon from being removed by the Senate.

America's Bicentennial celebration, the national celebration and relief of Sun-day, July 4, 1976's celebrations from Independence Mall in Philadelphia to the Na-tional Mall in Washington, D.C. and to backyards, beaches, barbeques, and fire-works across the United States that summer in 1976, brought the country a much-needed moment of pause and reflection. The celebration also brought a chance for America's Democrats and Republicans to catch their breath before what became one of the closest presidential contests of the twentieth century, one befitting the Bicentennial celebration with the return of nationally televised presidential debates between the Democrats and Republicans as well as the revival of the presidential primaries and caucuses. The year 1976 saw the culmination of years of state-by-state reform by both Democrats and Republicans to expand the presidential primary elections and caucuses. Some 30 primaries and caucuses opened the door to Republican former Gov. Ronald Reagan's party-splitting pri-mary challenge to Republican President Gerald R. Ford in the months before Au-gust 1976's Republican National Convention in Kansas City.[195] For Georgia's former Governor Jimmy Carter, the Democratic Party's caucuses and primaries allowed him to build a grassroots network of supporters whose successes pushed him to the front of a pack of some 15 other Democrats vying for the party's nod. Iowa's

---

appointment in his party and his willingness to think about doing the unimaginable: renaming the Republicans. "If that requires changing the name of the Republican Party, I'll even do that," Reagan said. "Reagan Says G.O.P. Needs New Name and New Support." *The Washington Post* Saturday, No-vember 20, 1976, 13.

195 "In two quick days last week, the Democrats wrapped it up and the Republicans didn't – and the great, exhausting experiment of the nation's new primary election system reached its conclu-sion," *Newsweek*'s Larry Martz reported in Monday, June 21, 1976's issue. "After 30 state primaries, more than $70,000,000.00 in campaign spending, millions of miles traveled and uncounted speeches given, that outcome was both anti-climactic and topsy-turvy. For the Democrats, the new system had worked better than most people had expected. The 30 primaries – nine more than had ever been held, a grueling test of political and physical stamina – had weeded out all but one of a field of candidates that numbered, all told, 13…For Republicans, on the other hand, the primaries proved more embarrassing than enlightening." Larry Martz, "Carter's Coup, Ford's Struggle." *News-week* 87, no. 26, Monday, June 21, 1976, 14 – 15.

Monday, January 19, 1976, Democratic caucuses, being used for their second time after being first introduced by the Democrats four years earlier in January 1972, underscored the importance of these state-by-state contests still further in a year that marked changes in the nomination process for both the Democrats and Republicans.

Monday evening, January 19, 1976's Iowa caucuses for the Democrats marked a historic election for former Gov. Jimmy Carter.[196] Carter's surprising win as a still-largely unknown Southern Democrat in the caucuses in Iowa thrust the former Governor into the nation's front-page headlines and solidified Iowa's caucusing in church basements and school gymnasiums to prominence for both parties in the nomination of their national tickets. Weeks later, Tuesday, February 24, 1976's New Hampshire primary saw the continued growth in stature of that state's primary into front-page stories in that year's start of the scramble for the Democratic and Republican presidential nominations. Carter's supporters from Georgia and elsewhere, calling themselves the Peanut Brigades, canvased both Iowa and New Hampshire in one of the most well-organized bids for support in these early nomination contests since Sen. Eugene McCarthy's young supporters in March 1968's New Hampshire Democratic primary.

Tuesday, November 3, 1976, an election with three nationally televised presidential debates as well as the first nationally televised Vice-Presidential debate, saw an election so close that it was not until almost four o'clock in the morning the next day on Wednesday, November 4, 1976, that the returns were clear. House and Senate majorities dating back to November 1954 held for the Democrats. Carter's 1976 victory was in the end incredibly close, the election of Carter barely against Ford a reminder of the resilience of the Republicans in a movement of scandal, near-impeachment, and resignation.

Four years after their 49-state defeat in November 1972, Democratic President-elect Jimmy Carter won the White House in a photo-finish election, one of the closest elections in the twentieth century, again, showing the resilience of the Democratic party just 4 years after winning just 1 state in Nixon's reelection. President-elect Jimmy Carter won a close Electoral vote majority over President Gerald R. Ford, the eighth sitting President in the history of the United States to be defeated in their bid for a second term in the White House. "Had there never been a Reagan candidacy in 1976, or had it all ended in North Carolina, Ford would have been elected in 1976," Ford White House strategist Harry Dent said later, as former Gov. Reagan's victories in some 11 state Republican presidential primaries were

---

196 "Iowa Dems Give Carter Lead in First U.S. Voter Test." *The Chicago Tribune* Tuesday, January 20, 1976, 5.

seen by the White House as figuring decisively in 1976's defeat of President Ford.[197] Still, the unpopularity of President Ford's Sunday, September 8, 1974 pardon of President Richard M. Nixon, his missteps and missed-opportunities by Ford in 1976's nationally televised debates, and the enthusiasm for President-elect Jimmy Carter's man-of-the-people appeal did much to tip the balance in a close race to the former Georgia Governor, an election in America's Bicentennial year of celebration of the history of America's Declaration of Independence and a country about to be challenged yet again with domestic and international crises for both the Democrats and Republicans.

---

197 Harry S. Dent, *The Prodigal South Returns to Power.* John Wiley and Sons, 1978, 55.

Chapter 6 The Democratic and Republican Parties in the New Century, 1980 – 2020

"We must act today in order to preserve tomorrow," the fortieth President of the United States said looking out from the sweeping vista of the Capitol Building's West Portico across the Washington, D.C. skyline. The National Mall was crowded on an unseasonably warm day in late January, "an almost balmy day," *The New York Times* told its readers. A crowd estimated at more than 500,000 people gathered below the "gleaming Presidential perch built onto the Capitol's west front" to watch President Ronald Reagan's Tuesday, January 20, 1981 Inauguration, "a well-timed flood of sunshine bathing him as he reached his inaugural peroration," the *Times* said.[198] It was the first such ceremony to be held on the Capitol's Western Portico on a specially-built scaffolding of seats and stages facing the National Mall, a western-facing ceremony fitting for the two-term Governor of California. With the thirty-ninth President and his family ready for their departure to travel back to their hometown of Plains at the ceremony's conclusion, President Jimmy Carter took in the same sweeping view of the cheering crowds on the National Mall and their applause of the words of his successor that Tuesday. The thirty-ninth President sat just a few feet away largely expressionless as Reagan recited the now-familiar failings that were to be a long-remembered legacy of the Carter White House.

"We have piled deficit upon deficit," Reagan told the crowd gathered at the Capitol and on the National Mall and those millions of Americans watching on TV in their homes that Tuesday. "We suffer from the longest and one of the worst sustained inflations in our national history," Reagan said. Carter, his Cabinet, and his administration had struggled to regain the American people's confidence and trust in their administration when its public approval slumped to a historic low of just 25% in July 1979. They'd lived every day with every financial statistic now being cited in the President's speech. "Idle industries have cast workers into unemployment, causing human misery and personal indignity," Reagan told the country. The growth in inflation and unemployment, the embargo of wheat and other agricultural exports to the Soviet Union, the shortages of gasoline at filling stations with lines of vehicles in every neighborhood, and the record-high in-

---

198 "Sun Smiles on the President, Blowing Kisses and Happy." *The New York Times* Wednesday, January 21, 1981, 28.

https://doi.org/10.1515/9783111340029-007

terest rates for home mortgages and business loans hit close to home for every American hearing the President speak that Tuesday.

"Next Tuesday," Reagan had asked voters months earlier on the evening of Tuesday, October 28, 1980 at the end of his only nationally televised debate with President Jimmy Carter, "all of you will go to the polls, will stand there in the polling place and make a decision. I think when you make that decision, it might be well if you would ask yourself, are you better off than you were four years ago? Is it easier for you to go and buy things in the stores than it was four years ago? Is there more or less unemployment in the country than there was four years ago?"[199] Exactly a week later, voters rendered their verdict. Tuesday, November 4, 1980 saw Reagan win 44 states and 489 Electoral votes, defeating President Jimmy Carter as the ninth sitting President to lose reelection. President-elect Reagan swept the once-solid Democratic South, except for Carter's home state of Georgia. Reagan and his running-mate George H.W. Bush ran up the score in the West, including Reagan's state of California, won with almost 53% of the vote.[200] In the East, Reagan and Bush won in traditionally Democratic states, including Massachusetts and New York.

The ninety-seventh Congress, sworn-in days before President Reagan's Inauguration, kept a solid Democratic House majority and kept Speaker of the House Tip O'Neill at the rostrum. In the House, Democrats held their majority for the full eight-years of Reagan's two-terms in the White House, continuing the longest party majority in the history of either chamber of Congress. Democrats lost their Senate majority, with twelve new Republican Senators elected that Tuesday, including Sen. Mack Mattingly who'd defeated Democratic Sen. Herman Talmadge in President Carter's home state of Georgia.[201]

In the early months of 1981, President Reagan revived a Republican Party that Reagan himself just four or so years earlier had asked audiences whether it would survive the Watergate controversy and the resignation of President Nixon. "Reagan Says G.O.P. Needs New Name and New Support," *The Washington Post*'s Saturday November 20, 1976 headline had told the *Post*'s readers just four years earlier.[202] Republicans in the mid-1970s were so deep in debt as a national party, as Speaker Tip O'Neill shared in his 1987 memoirs, *Man of the House: The Life and Political*

199 "Carter, Reagan Clash on Peace and Economy, Anderson, from 300 Miles Away, Disagrees with Both." *The Chicago Tribune* Wednesday, October 29, 1980, 1.
200 "Vote for President by States." *The New York Times* Thursday, November 6, 1980, 28.
201 "Mattingly Outruns Talmadge by 22,008." *The Atlanta Constitution* Thursday, November 6, 1980, 1.
202 "Reagan Says G.O.P. Needs New Name and New Support." *The Washington Post* Saturday, November 20, 1976, 13.

Memoirs of Speaker Tip O'Neill, that they offered to sell their Capitol Hill Club at 300 First St. SE to the Democrats.[203] Now, in January 1981, the Reagan White House stood at a moment of reinvigoration of the Republicans, with the Republicans flush with millions of dollars to spend on their well-run national campaigns.

In the first months of the Reagan White House, conservative Democrats in the House and Senate were wooed by Reagan to break with their Congressional leadership and back the President's tax bill, with behind-the-scenes work by the White House to court conservative Democrats, a few of whom later switched parties to the Republicans. House and Senate Democrats, including Democratic Rep. Kent Hance of Texas' nineteenth House district who'd defeated Republican George W. Bush for that seat in 1978's midterms, and others backed the White House in the weeks prior to bill's final passage in July. "As long as people are going to support him, he's not going to go out and campaign against them," White House Chief of Staff James A. Baker said, as the White House confirmed that House and Senate Democrats supporting 1981's tax measure would not face campaigning against them by the President in their reelections.[204]

"Republicans Meet Setbacks in House, Several Losses in Key Races Threaten Reagan Coalition," *The New York Times* told its readers the morning after 1982's midterms, when the White House's deficit-trimming, tax-cutting promises crashed into the recession-ravaged realities of the country, especially the hard-hit rural towns of the Midwest and South. Farm foreclosures, homelessness, and unemployment gripped the country months before 1982's midterms. Hardships of millions of households barely making ends-meet shored up support for the Democrats in forcing the hand of the White House for an aisle-crossing renewal of the New Deal's social contract with generations of American families. Beginning that December, Democrats on Capitol Hill turned their attention to shoring-up of the Depression-born New Deal promise made to America's seniors with their strengthened majorities in Congress after November's midterms.

"Today," President Reagan told an audience on the South Lawn of the White House on Wednesday, April 20, 1983, "we reaffirm Franklin Roosevelt's commitment that Social Security must always provide a secure and stable base so that

---

203 "Not so long ago, when [Gerald] Ford was President, the Republican Party was so broke that they actually offered to sell their Capitol Hill club to the Democrats," Speaker O'Neill later wrote. "But now, only five years later, [Republicans] had hundreds of millions of dollars to spend on campaigns not to mention an impressive party organization." Tip O'Neill, *Man of the House: The Life and Political Memoirs of Speaker Tip O'Neill.* The Bodley Head, 1987, 338.
204 "White House Soliciting Tax Support." *The New York Times* Saturday, June 6, 1981, 1, 30.

older Americans may live in dignity." [205] From a stage filled with Congressional Democrats led by Speaker of the House Tip O'Neill, House Ways and Means Chair Rep. Dan Rostenkowski of Illinois, Senator Claude Pepper of Florida, and others, Reagan spoke of Social Security, in the President's words, as "a monument to the spirit of compassion and commitment that unites us as a people." Reagan spoke admiringly of Franklin Roosevelt's promise to protect the well-being of America's elderly, as Reagan signed his own measure extending the life of the New Deal program, in part, by changes to the federal payroll tax and by changes in the eligibility and retirement age for full-benefits. [206] "We've restored some much needed security to an uncertain world," Reagan said, thanking the House and Senate Democrats and Republicans who worked on the bill for months after 1982's midterms, a far cry from the government-is-the-problem vision presented just two years earlier at his Inauguration.

Tuesday, November 6, 1984's election saw President Reagan and Vice President George H.W. Bush defeat former Vice President Walter Mondale, whose selection of then-Rep. Geraldine Ferraro of New York's ninth House District as his Vice President energized Democrats across the country as the first woman ever selected to run on a Democratic or Republican national ticket. [207] The White House left little to chance in an election where it led the Democrats in every poll for months, with Reagan traveling across the country, appearing in two nationally televised presidential debates with Mondale, and relentless fundraising for commercial spots reaching millions of American TV viewers. Reagan fell short of a 50-state sweep by a mere 3,761 votes in Mondale's state of Minnesota. [208] Reagan's reelection took a page from the Democrats' playbook in a series of speeches from the rear-platform of the same railroad car used by President Harry Truman in his 1948 re-election. Reagan told railyard audiences in Ohio of his admiration for President Truman, as local high-school bands played the traditional Democratic anthem, "Happy Days Are Here Again." [209] Republicans picked up more than a dozen seats in the House of Representatives, nowhere close to a Republican majority

---

205 "Pension Changes Signed into Law, Social Security Rescue Hailed by President at Ceremony on White House Lawn." *The New York Times* Thursday, April 21, 1983, 17.

206 "President, on a Note of Bipartisanship, Signs Social Security Bill." *The Washington Post* Thursday, April 21, 1983, 10.

207 "Geraldine Ferraro is Chosen by Mondale as Running Mate, First Woman on Major Ticket, 'Difficult' Decision, But Likely Nominee Says Representative from Queens is 'Best.'" *The New York Times* Friday, July 13, 1984, 1.

208 "Reagan's Margin is 16,876,932 Votes, President's Popular Vote Lead Second Biggest in History, Official Tallies Show." *The New York Times* Saturday, December 22, 1984, 10.

209 "Ron Gives 'Em Some of Harry's Hell." *The Chicago Tribune* Saturday, October 13, 1984, 3.

in the House but still an inroad into a Democratic House majority dating back to the first term of the Eisenhower administration.

In the face of 1984's 49 state sweep for Reagan, an influential group of Democratic lawmakers on Capitol Hill were reenergized to revive the Democratic Party. Democrats were only weeks from finishing construction of their permanent national headquarters on a tree-shaded street just a few blocks from the Capitol. Democrats built their permanent national headquarters just a short walk from the Capitol, allowing House and Senate Democrats and their staff to easily use the offices for campaign strategy sessions, production of TV commercials, and fundraising telephone-calls to donors.[210] When construction was completed on the Democrats' new building in January 1985, Democrats and Republicans would be just a few minutes' walk from each other on Capitol Hill, the Republicans directly across the street from the Cannon House Office Building and the Democrats just down the street and around the corner on South Capitol St., both with modern facilities to house their staff and to operate their media production studios, polling operations, and fundraising staff, all to serve the reelection of incumbent House and Senate members just a short walk from their offices on Capitol Hill and to coordinate with candidates in presidential campaigns.

With dangerously-cold temperatures in Washington, D.C. on Sunday, January 20, 1985, President Reagan's second Inauguration was held indoors with no Inaugural parade and little of the traditional fanfare and crowds. A small televised ceremony from the White House for the President and his family took place on Sunday, January 20, 1985 and then a larger second ceremony was held in the Capitol Rotunda on Monday, January 21, 1985. As Republicans celebrated their successes in their 49-state sweep for the President's reelection and celebrated holding their majority in the Senate, Democratic National Committee (DNC) leaders gathered in the capital just a few days later to chart their party's future in growing their ranks and reassessing their strategies to build the party in a second Reagan term. Taking a break from their meetings on Thursday, January 31, 1985 during a three-day session of the DNC, party leaders took time from their meetings to dedicate the Democratic Party's new permanent national headquarters at 430 South Capitol St. just a few blocks from the Capitol.[211] Within weeks, Democrats took more steps to rebuilding their ranks on Capitol Hill and in presidential elections in the launch of the Democratic Leadership Council (DLC).

---

210 "Democrats Building Capitol Hill Headquarters." *The Washington Post* Saturday, April 23, 1983, F3.

211 "Vote Aids Kennedy Ally's Effort to Head Democratic Committee." *The New York Times* Friday, February 1, 1985, 19.

"Dissidents Defy Top Democrats, Council Formed," *The New York Times* front-page story told its readers on Friday, March 1, 1985 as months of meetings by House and Senate Democrats, Democratic Governors, Mayors, and others culminated in a Capitol Hill press conference announcing the formation of the Democratic Leadership Council (DLC), a reform-minded group aimed at rebuilding the Democrats nationally and at reinvigorating the party in the wake of the 49-state loss to Reagan.[212] DLC founding-members included Senator Sam Nunn of Georgia, Rep. Richard A. Gephardt of Missouri, Sen. Lawton Chiles of Florida, and others who brought heft to the organization, expanding its ranks to include Gov. Dale Bumpers of Arkansas, Rep. Jim Wright of Texas, Rep. Jim Cooper of Tennessee, and a rising star in DLC ranks, Gov. Bill Clinton of Arkansas, who delivered the Democratic Party's rebuttal to President Reagan's Wednesday, February 6, 1985 State of the Union Address. Democratic successes in 1986's midterms, that saw Democrats hold their majority in the House, and, more importantly, winning back the Democratic majority in the Senate, brought a new energy to the Democrats going into the 1988 race.

Tuesday, November 8, 1988's election pitting then-Vice President George H.W. Bush against Gov. Michael Dukakis of Massachusetts was a turning-point in campaigning in presidential elections at the end of the twentieth century. A sharpening of attacks took place in 1988 with a more adversarial-oriented tone in the TV commercials aired by the Democrats and Republicans that felt and looked different in so many ways from 1984's presidential election. Sharp-edged negative advertising in network TV broadcasts, cable TV, and radio commercials aired by the campaigns of then-Vice President Bush and Gov. Dukakis. 1988 changed presidential campaigns for Democrats and Republicans, with TV ads mirroring a sharply and starkly polarized country and with declining voter turnout only elevating the sharper, more strident voices in the Democratic and Republican ranks.[213] The newly-emerging technologies in cable and satellite TV and in the harnessing of computers amplified less the voices of moderation so long heard for Democrats and Republicans in the nation's newspapers and coast-to-coast network TV, replaced by the more extreme voices of those who'd be more readily heard on the din of cable TV, A.M. talk-radio, and on direct mail fundraising. All of this new technology in 1988's race drove and divided the Democrats and Republicans in ways that reverberated well-into the twenty-first century.

Wednesday, July 21, 1988's nationally televised speech from Atlanta's Democratic National Convention in the Omni Coliseum by then-Gov. Bill Clinton of Ar-

---

212 "Dissidents Defy Top Democrats, Council Formed, More Conservative Line is Goal of Policy Panel." *The New York Times* Friday, March 1, 1985, 1.
213 "Nominees Wage Intensified War of Attack Ads." *The New York Times* Monday, October 10, 1988, 1.

kansas, as delegates awaited the appearance of Gov. Dukakis that Wednesday evening, became an unexpected moment in the rising profile of a figure closely associated with the DLC and the New Democrats, as they called themselves. Network TV anchors, reporters on the convention floor of the Omni Coliseum, and the hundreds of reporters filing their bylines from downtown Atlanta that Wednesday night made light of the Gov.'s longwinded speech and reported the jeers of delegates from the floor, as a nationally-televised speech scheduled to last an allotted 15-minutes continued for almost 33-minutes with delegates chanting "DUKE, DUKE, DUKE" for Gov. Dukakis that sounded like booing on the network broadcast, along with air-horns and yelling from the delegates. The normally polished and smooth-speaking Clinton appeared annoyed with his fellow delegates. For the last few minutes of his remarks, the Governor almost shouted the closing few minutes of his speech. "I want you to quiet down so I can tell the rest of the country why they should like Mike," Clinton admonished the Democratic delegates in Atlanta. ABC producers aired a live-shot from over the shoulder of Clinton showing a flashing red-light from convention managers through the closing minutes of the speech.[214] Meanwhile, cutaway shots of convention delegates that Wednesday evening in prime-time network broadcasts from the floor of the Omni Coliseum showed many shaking their heads, yelling, and gesturing thumbs-down during the Governor's remarks.

Days later, on Thursday evening, July 28, 1988, millions of television viewers of NBC's *The Tonight Show* starring Johnny Carson saw the Arkansas Gov. step on to Carson's famous set on the stage in Burbank, California. Days after his Democratic National Convention embarrassment, Gov. Bill Clinton appeared in a damage-controlling guest-appearance, laughing at his Atlanta speech and even playing the saxophone with *The Tonight Show*'s Doc Severinsen and the NBC Orchestra. With Doc Severinsen and the orchestra performing a rousing rendition of "Happy Days Are Here Again" as the Arkansas Gov. walked out and sat down next to *The Tonight Show*'s Ed McMahon, Clinton laughed and joked his way through the next 15-minutes.

"The truth is, I did it on purpose, I always wanted to be on this show in the worst way," Clinton joked with Carson. "It was awful, it was awful. What can I tell you, it went from bad to worse," Clinton said, making light of his own speech at the Omni Coliseum in Atlanta. "I tell you what worked for you, you've got a sense of humor, and that probably is one of the great saving graces of people who are in public office, a lot of them don't have a sense of humor," *The Tonight*

---

214 "Gov. Clinton Wears Out Welcome with Nominating Speech." *The Washington Post* Thursday, July 21, 1988, 27.

Show's Johnny Carson said in complimenting the Governor, giving the rising star in the ranks of Democratic Governors and a prominent figure in the newly-formed DLC a face-saving appearance in Burbank, California with a TV viewing audience many times larger than those likely to have tuned in and watched his 33-minute speech from Atlanta a week earlier.

"Hey, Governor, do you have enough air left to blow this thing?" Doc Severinsen asked Gov. Clinton as he finished with Carson, as Clinton sprinted across the stage in the Burbank studio and played a rendition of "Summertime" on the saxophone handed to him by Severinsen. "Does this mean we have to offer a Republican Governor equal time musically?" Carson joked. What Clinton did that Thursday evening, July 28, 1988 in Burbank, California on the set of *The Tonight Show* is what today is the well-worn path for Democrats and Republicans to the stages, studios, and production-sets of popular, more entertainment-themed programs from New York City to Los Angeles, California and everywhere in between.

Tuesday, November 8, 1988's split-the difference election of President George H.W. Bush and Democratic House and Senate majorities marked the divisions so dominant in that year's presidential election.[215] Bush carried California as the last Republican presidential ticket to carry that state in a presidential election, but didn't win a Republican majority in either the House or the Senate as just the third President in history elected without carrying either chamber in Congress, in company with President Zachary Taylor and President Richard Nixon.[216] Bush ended what some of his own advisors called the Van Buren curse, as the 1st sitting Vice President elected since 1836 and just the 4th in history to be elected from the Vice Presidency to the Presidency.

World-changing events to come, from the collapse of the Soviet Union and regimes in Eastern Europe to the international outcry after Iraq's August 1990 invasion of Kuwait, all played themselves out in 1988's election and after. For the Bush White House, the rise of the American public's approval for Bush in February 1991 (89 % approval, Gallup reported) with the Gulf War and then its free-fall to a low of just 29 % approval in July 1992 were the roller-coaster of 1991 and 1992. For Democrats, a tier of candidates fearful of facing a wartime incumbent in the White House with the soaring approval ratings of President Bush in early 1991 pushed so many Democrats away from their bids for the White House by the end of

---

215 "Bush Is Elected President, Democrats Maintain Firm Control of U.S. House and Senate, Dukakis Tells his Supporters, 'We'll Work with Him.'" *The Chicago Tribune* Wednesday, November 9, 1988, 1.

216 "Democrats Keep Solid Hold on Congress." *The New York Times* Wednesday, November 9, 1988, 24.

1991 that a still-relatively little-known Democratic Governor stepped forward when so many Democrats had stepped back for 1992's presidential contest.

"I refuse to be part of a generation of Americans that celebrates the death of Communism abroad with the loss of the American dream at home," then-Gov. Bill Clinton said from the tree-shaded steps of the old Arkansas statehouse in Little Rock, Arkansas on Thursday, October 3, 1991. "Make no mistake, this election is about change. Change in our party, change in our leadership, change in our nation, and that is why today I proudly announce my candidacy for President of the United States of America," Clinton said at the old Arkansas statehouse, in announcing his bid for the Democratic nomination, just days after then-Senator Al Gore announced his decision not to run for the Democratic presidential nomination.[217]

With then-Gov. Bill Clinton's victories in Democratic presidential primaries in California, New Jersey, and Ohio clinching the Democratic nomination – "the election for America's future begins tomorrow," Clinton told a group of supporters that Tuesday evening in Los Angeles, California – Tuesday, November 3, 1992's election took any number of turns and twists in a race that included not only Republican President George H.W. Bush, but a wealthy Texas businessman, H. Ross Perot, seemingly prepared to spend vast sums of his own money for his independent bid for the White House.[218] Clinton's selection of Tennessee Senator Al Gore and a successful Democratic National Convention in New York City's Madison Square Garden prompted Perot to announce his withdrawal at a Dallas press conference. Perot's announcement that Thursday electrified the Democratic National Convention still meeting in Madison Square Garden.

"Now that the Democratic Party has revitalized itself, I have concluded that we cannot win in November," Perot told reporters at his Dallas press conference on the morning of Thursday, July 16, 1992. "The Democratic Party has revitalized itself, they've done a brilliant job, in my opinion, in coming back," Perot told reporters, thanking his campaign's volunteers and applauding their state-by-state drives for gathering signatures in petitions qualifying Perot for the ballot. "I believe it would be disruptive for us to continue," Perot said that Thursday morning, and said he wasn't going to endorse either President George H.W. Bush or Gov. Clinton even as he praised the Democratic Party.

---

217 "Arkansas' Clinton Enters the '92 Race for President." *The New York Times* Friday, October 4, 1991, 10.
218 "Clinton Wins a Majority for Nomination but Perot's Appeal Is Strong in Two Parties, Final Six Primaries, Easy Victories for Bush Diluted by Signs of Outsider's Power." *The New York Times* Wednesday, July 3, 1992, 1, 16.

Weeks later, on Friday, October 1, 1992, in yet another turn and twist to the election, Perot resumed his independent campaign for the White House. Volunteers had kept working after July's announcement to collect enough signatures to qualify Perot on the ballot in all 50 states.[219] In another press conference from Dallas, Perot resumed his candidacy for the White House, telling reporters "the volunteers in all 50 states have asked me to run as a candidate for President of the United States, Jim Stockdale, our Vice Presidential candidate, and I are honored to accept their request." "I know I hurt many of the volunteers who worked so hard through the spring and summer when I stepped aside in July," Perot told the reporters in Dallas. "I thought it was the right thing to do, I thought that both political parties would address the problems that face the nation, we gave them a chance, they didn't do it," Perot said. Meeting the polling threshold of at least 15% set by the Commission on Presidential Debates (CPD), H. Ross Perot and his running mate, retired U.S. Navy Vice Admiral James B. Stockdale, prepared for 3 televised presidential debates with Bush and Clinton and a Vice Presidential debate with Gore and Vice President Dan Quayle.

Tuesday, November 3, 1992's election was unlike any other in recent history. In the end, Governor Clinton carried 32 states and won 370 Electoral votes to defeat Bush, the tenth sitting President to lose their bid for reelection. Even as he won some 18.89% of the vote nationally and carried an estimated 19,725,433 votes in his bid for the White House, Perot fell far short of winning the Electoral votes of any state in the United States.[220] Exit polls later showed that had Perot not been on the ballot, most of Perot's voters in most states would've been almost evenly-split their ballots between President Bush and President-elect Clinton.[221] Impossible in hindsight is knowing how much larger and more impactful H. Ross Perot's candidacy might have proven had he not erratically and unexpectedly suspended his bid during the Democratic National Convention in New York City.

---

219 "Perot Re-Enters the Campaign, Saying Bush and Clinton Fail to Address Government 'Mess,' Faces Lag in Polls, Negotiators for Parties Report Agreement on Series of Debates." *The New York Times* Friday, October 2, 1992, 1.

220 "Election Turnout Highest since '68, 55.23% Figure is Attributed Mostly to Perot's Appeal, Except in the South." *The New York Times* Thursday, December 17, 1992, B16.

221 "The impact of Mr. Perot's supporters on the campaign's outcome appears to have been minimal," *The New York Times*' Steven Holmes told readers. "If Mr. Perot had not been on the ballot, 38% of his voters said they would have voted for Gov. Bill Clinton, and 38% said they would have voted for President Bush." Of Perot's voters, 14% said pollsters they would have cast their vote for any other independent candidate on the ballot. "An Eccentric but No Joke, Perot's Strong Showing Raises Questions on What Might Have Been, and Might Be." *The New York Times* Thursday, November 5, 1992, B4.

"G.O.P. Captures Congress," *The Washington Post*'s Wednesday, November 9, 1994, headlines told readers of the historic Republican midterm, with the win of over fifty House seats and at least eight Senate races by Republicans. "Party Controls Both Houses for the First Time Since '50s," the *Post*'s headline said. 1994's midterms marked a defeat for the Clinton White House, which lost the House and Senate largely over the failed Health Security Act.[222] 1994's midterms began a House and Senate majority that held for the Republicans through the reelection of President George W. Bush to his second-term in November 2004. Republican majorities held in the House and Senate for the remainder of the Clinton White House, including 1996's reelection of Republican House and Senate majorities in a split-the-difference election with the reelection of Clinton to a second-term.[223] Republicans held the House and Senate through 1998's midterms, kept Congress in November 2000's cliffhanger election between then-Governor George W. Bush and then-Vice President Al Gore, held onto the House in 2002's midterms (and won back the Senate after losing it temporarily to the Democrats in 2001 when Sen. Jim Jeffords of Vermont left the Republicans), and kept the House and Senate for Republicans in November 2004's reelection of President George W. Bush. Not until 2006's midterms did the Democrats finally win back House and Senate at a time of setbacks and stumbles for the Bush White House in its second term.

From Tuesday, November 7, 2000's county-by-county and precinct-by-precinct fight between then-Vice President Al Gore and then-Gov. George W. Bush in Florida through Tuesday, November 3, 2020's election with the defeat of President Donald J. Trump by former Vice President Joe Biden, campaigns fought by the Democrats and the Republicans in the start of the twenty-first century have been as close-to-the-wire and hard-fought as any in the country's history.[224] Twenty-first century cutting-edge technologies in marketing, data mining, and ever more precise analysis of tracking voter turnout are intermingled with a sharp-edged, sharp-elbowed partisanship and a bitter polarization throwing back to the earliest days of some of the country's most hard-fought clashes in the history of presidential elections. In a twenty-first century that has shown the campaigns of the Democrats and the Republicans to be ever more adept at adapting cutting-edge technologies to reach an ever more dispersed, distrustful, and distracted electorate, it is a time when elec-

---

222 "G.O.P. Offers a 'Contract' to Revive Reagan Years." *The Washington Post* Wednesday, September 28, 1994, 1.

223 "Clinton Elected to a Second Term with Solid Margins Across U.S., G.O.P. Keeps Hold on Congress, Democrats Fail to Reverse Right's Capitol Hill Gains." *The New York Times* Wednesday, November 6, 1996, 1.

224 Rachel Bitecofer, "Fear Factor: The Hidden Dynamic That's Transformed Our Politics, and Will Loom Large in the 2020 Race." *The New Republic* Sunday, March 1, 2020, 28 – 37.

tions to the White House may still turn on as few as 30 or so counties in perhaps just half a dozen or so states, as Democrats and Republicans spend unprecedented sums of money and time chiseling away at a persuadable 5%, or even as little as 2% or 1% of undecided voters in a smaller, angrier electorate in most elections today.

When surveyed by Gallup in January and February 2021 and asked "In your view, do the Republican and Democratic parties do an adequate job of representing the American people, or do they do such a poor job that a third major party is needed?" those surveyed by Gallup just weeks after Tuesday, November 3, 2020's election said by a margin of 62% to 33% that a third major party is needed to take on the Democrats and Republicans, an increase from a margin of 57% in September 2020 weeks before the November contest. Support for a third party has fluctuated between 57% and 62% since October 2013, according to Gallup.[225] And yet, Democrats and Republicans find themselves facing fewer independent or third party bids in the twenty-first century in the era of hyper-partisan, hyper-polarized elections. An estimated 19,725,433 Americans cast their votes for H. Ross Perot in 1992's election, but Perot's second bid in 1996 won fewer than half of his bid four-years earlier.[226] Few independent bids have done anywhere as well since 1996. Americans may tell pollsters they'd like a choice other than the Democrats or Republicans on the ballot, but elections from 2000 through 2020 remind us how easily Democrats and Republicans still deflect independent candidacies. Large percentages of Americans tell pollsters they want a third party alternative, but barely and rarely do they cast their votes today this way.

From 2000's Florida hanging-chads cliffhanger through 2020's socially-distanced presidential contest, elections in the early years of the twenty-first century have had their share of history-making moments, moments more and more seen not on the screens of TV sets in family rooms and living rooms by family and friends, but in the palm-sized screens of cell-phones.[227] 2008's election of President

---

225 Gallup News Service, *January Wave One, Final Topline*, results based on telephone interviews conducted between Thursday, January 21, 2021 and Tuesday, February 2, 2021 with a random sample of 906 adults, ages 18 and older, living in all 50 states and the District of Columbia, conducted with respondents on landline telephones and cellular phones.

226 "Perot Supporters Concentrate on Their Goals for the Future." *The New York Times* Wednesday, November 6, 1996, 34.

227 Writing in 2008's *The Big Sort: Why the Clustering of Like-Minded America Is Tearing Us Apart*, Bill Bishop offers insight into this moment. "Beginning nearly 30 years ago, the people of this country unwittingly began a social experiment," Bishop says. "We have created, and are creating, new institutions distinguished by their isolation and single-mindedness," Bishop tells us. "We have replaced a belief in a nation with a trust in ourselves and our carefully chosen surroundings. And we have worked quietly and hard to remove any trace of the 'constant clashing of opinions' from daily

Barack Obama in that contest defeating Senator John McCain of Arizona and his
Vice Presidential running-mate, then-Governor Sarah Palin of Alaska, whiplashed
Americans who went from celebrating the history-making moment of President
Obama's election to the blowback and brushback against the Obama White
House and the Democrats over March 2010's Affordable Care Act. The shellacking,
as President Obama put it, when Republicans won their House majority in Novem-
ber 2010 whiplashed back to the reelection of President Obama in November 2012.
President Obama's 2012 reelection seemed every bit as uneventful as 2004's reelection of President George W. Bush. 2010's midterm loss of the House for the Obama
White House born of the pent-up frustrations of Republicans seemed every bit as
familiar as 2018's midterm loss for the Republicans to fed-up Democrats angered at
the Trump White House.

Tuesday, November 8, 2016, and Tuesday, November 3, 2020, were both some of
the most volatile elections in a time of change and challenge for Democrats and
Republicans at the start of the twenty-first century, back-to-back roiling elections
with little of the relative stability of, say, 2004's reelection of President George
W. Bush or 2012's reelection of President Barack Obama. 2016 is perhaps most
well-remembered by Democrats and Republicans alike as an election of the
Web-browser, as millions of Americans spent hours hitting refresh on sites like
The New York Times' election Webpage or Nate Silver's *538*, tracking the performance and polling of Democratic presidential nominee Hillary Clinton and Republican Donald J. Trump. Michigan, Pennsylvania, Wisconsin, the so-called blue-wall
states watched closely in the closing days of Tuesday, November 8, 2016's election,
all three barely broke by less than one percent each and by a combined vote of an
estimated 107,330 votes for President-elect Donald J. Trump and Vice President-elect
Mike Pence.[228] Democratic disappointments deepened as Clinton campaign strategists watched the popular vote nationally inch up day-by-day until settling at an
estimated 2,868,519 more votes cast nationally for former Sen. Clinton and her running mate, Sen. Tim Kaine of Virginia. For the second time in less than 20 years'
time, and for no less than at least the third time in the history of the Democrats
and Republicans, the Democratic national ticket had carried the popular vote nationally yet not won the state-by-state combination of enough states for an Electoral vote majority.

life," he says. "Now more isolated than ever in our private lives, cocooned with our fellows, we
approach life with the sensibility of customers who are always right," Bishop says. Bill Bishop,
The Big Sort: Why the Clustering of Like-Minded America Is Tearing Us Apart. Houghton Mifflin
Company, 2008, 302 – 303.
228 Jonathan Allen and Amie Parnes, *Shattered: Inside Hillary Clinton's Doomed Campaign.*
Crown, 2017, 381.

Friday, January 20, 2017's Inauguration of President Donald J. Trump on the West Portico of the Capitol Building set a characteristically unhinged tone – "Well, that was some weird shit," President George W. Bush reportedly said that Friday as he left the ceremony's stage at the Capitol – and marked a moment of weeks of peaceful protests and lawsuits over immigration and some of the early initiatives of the Trump White House.[229] In the first days of the Trump White House, Democrats and Republicans in Congress circled-back to some of the same debates that sparked the earliest disagreements and laid the first foundations for the first political parties in the first Congress gaveling into session in April 1789: immigration, trade, and tariffs. 2018's midterms with the election of a House Democratic majority, the so-called blue-wave campaign where Democratic House candidates successfully reached voters in longtime, onetime Republican strongholds like California's Orange County and in Georgia's Cobb County, and the return of Rep. Nancy Pelosi to serve in her second term as Speaker of the House made history still months later with the impeachment of President Donald J. Trump.

Tuesday, November 3, 2020, was anything but an election like normal, as the COVID-19 pandemic and social distancing upended decades of forecasting, predictive modeling, and journalistic punditry. In the early months of 2020, an improbable sequence of events following 2020's Iowa caucuses and 2020's New Hampshire primary culminated somewhat unexpectedly in South Carolina's 2020 presidential primary where a last-minute surge by former Vice President Joe Biden (helped with the endorsement of South Carolina's Rep. James Clyburn) led the Democrats to a rallying of Democratic rivals to former Vice President Biden's candidacy. Months later, a flurry of predictions that former Vice President Joe Biden and his running-mate, then-Senator Kamala Harris of California had squandered time in ineffective online and social media appearances by the former Vice President from his home in Wilmington, Delaware were replaced by a burst of activity by the Democratic national ticket, and by the disarray of President Trump's campaign and the difficulties of Trump in building much-needed momentum in his signature rallies that had proven to be such a successful part of his November 2016 bid. President Barack Obama took on a far more active role in months of campaigning alongside former Vice President Biden than any former President against his sitting successor in recent memory. In contrast to President Bill Clinton's distance from 2000's election and President George W. Bush's largely stepping off-

229 Tim Alberta, *American Carnage: On the Front Lines of the Republican Civil War and the Rise of President Trump.* HarperCollins, 2019, 425.

stage in 2008's election, President Obama's campaigning against his sitting successor's seeking a 2nd term made Tuesday, November 3, 2020 an election like no other.

When the dust settled on Tuesday, November 3, 2020, President-elect Joe Biden and Vice-President-elect Kamala Harris made history in winning one of the most remarkable elections in decades, with President Donald J. Trump defeated as the eleventh sitting President to lose in running for reelection to a second term. For the first time in the history of the United States, an impeached President ran for reelection, and lost in their bid for a second term in the White House. With the collapse of President Trump's reelection campaign in its disorganization paralleled in the collapse in the Trump White House in its disarray in the federal government's response to the COVID-19 pandemic, President-elect Joe Biden's election in Tuesday, November 3, 2020 might be mistakenly made to be a foregone conclusion. However, in retrospect, it was every bit the close-to-the-wire election that rattled the country four-years earlier in Tuesday, November 8, 2016's election.[230]

Had the Democratic Party not coalesced around former Vice President Biden when it did in Saturday, February 29, 2020's South Carolina Democratic primary, had President Trump spent less time infighting in his own administration's disarrayed ranks in the response to the COVID-19 pandemic, had President Trump's campaign organization been more stable, had President Barack Obama declined to take such an active involvement in former Vice President Biden's campaign, had even a few of these dynamics been different in that extraordinary year, the Trump White House very well might have narrowly won reelection to a second term in spite of the public's unhappiness with the day-to-day work on the COVID-19 pandemic response and recovery from President Trump.

For many Democrats, exhaling on Tuesday, November 3, 2020, came in winning the White House and in holding the House of Representatives, but excitement still was a few months away with the historic moment in the election of a Democratic Senate in two of the most extraordinary campaigns for that chamber in its history, both in the now-battleground state of Georgia. Tuesday, January 5, 2021's runoffs in the state of Georgia were a series of striking events thanks to that state's unique general election runoff requirement. The runoff in a special non-partisan primary for Senator Kelly Loeffler's seat was a foregone conclusion. With the strong candidacy of the Reverend Raphael Warnock as well as the Republican-splitting bid of former Rep. Doug Collins ensuring no candidate received the 50% requirement in the non-partisan primary, Loeffler's January runoff was expected. Sen. Loeffler and the Rev. Warnock went on to Tuesday, January 5, 2021's non-partisan primary

---

230 Jonathan Allen and Amie Parnes, *Lucky: How Joe Biden Barely Won the Presidency.* Random House, 2021.

runoff exactly as expected. Tuesday, November 3, 2020's truly historic upset in the Peach State came in Sen. David Perdue's falling below Georgia's 50% general election runoff requirement, thanks to the showing of Georgia's Libertarian Senate candidate Shane Hazel. Ineffective campaigning by President Donald Trump in the Peach State in the weeks before Tuesday, January 5, 2021's runoffs and the energetic campaigning of President-elect Joe Biden and Democratic leaders won Senate seats for the Reverend Raphael Warnock and Democrat Jon Ossoff, and won a historic 50 – 50 Senate working-majority for the Democrats starting in January 2021 for the Biden White House.

"We're going to walk down, and I'll be there with you, we're going to walk down to the Capitol, and we're going to cheer on our brave Senators and Congressmen and women, and we're probably not going to be cheering so much for some of them, because you'll never take back our country with weakness, you have to show strength, you have to be strong," President Trump told thousands of his supporters in Washington, D.C. gathered in front of a stage adorned with a large banner overhead with the words SAVE AMERICA MARCH on the Ellipse just to the south of the White House. The day was Wednesday, January 6, 2021.[231] In a House of Representatives chamber still rattled and still reeling by the ransacking of the thousands who'd stormed it a week earlier, Democratic leaders took a step without precedent in the nation's history to impeach the President of the United States a week later on Wednesday, January 13, 2021 for incitement to insurrection of thousands of his supporters whose trash still lay strewn in waste-cans and hallway-corners of the Capitol as the House tallied its impeachment votes.[232] President Trump was impeached for the second time, the first time ever that a President had been impeached twice in the history of the United States. Wednesday, January 20, 2021's peaceful transfer of power in the Inauguration of President Joe Biden and Vice President Kamala Harris took place on the West Portico of the Capitol Building in a setting anything but peaceful just two weeks earlier, the Capitol and the country still reeling from Insurrection and impeachment. Trump's flight lifted off from Washington, D.C. shortly after 8:50 A.M. The twice-impeached forty-fifth President of the United States, one who'd promised just three weeks earlier he'd "walk down" to the Capitol, was now miles from it.

---

231 "Americans at the Gates: The Trump Era's Inevitable Denouement." *The New York Times* Thursday, January 2, 2021, 1.
232 "Trump Impeached Again, 232 to 197, Senate Trial Is Likely to Occur After Departure." *The Washington Post* Thursday, January 14, 2021, 1.

Chapter 7 Negative Partisanship, Performative Partisanship, and the 2024 Presidential Election and Beyond

When we take a step back and take the longer view of our history of presidential campaigning from the earliest elections of the 1790s through the early decades of the 21st century, it is defined as much as it has ever been around the hyper-partisan, bitterly polarized campaigning for our nation's highest offices. Today, some of the leading scholars in political science tell us that most voters cast their votes against a candidate they dislike, as much as for one that they favor.

The theory of negative partisanship is leading the way in the study of campaigning in the United States today, as we know that most voters cast their votes against a candidate they fear or hate as much as for one that they like. Fitted to a day when most voters in their scrolling and swiping on digital platforms and social media see their favored candidates warning with urgency of stopping the other side from winning at the polls, the theory of negative partisanship is a framework for understanding our own day's unrelentingly adversarial campaigning. Candidates and their appeals to voters are most clearly centered not by telling their supporters what they're for, as much as reminding them who they're against and what they dislike about the other candidate. In the digitally-driven daily lives of most Americans, candidates find their success not in the messaging of what they stand for as much as in reminding voters of the sharp and stark differences they have with their rivals.

"Voters are more motivated to defeat the other side than by any particular policy goals," David Freelander tells us, as campaigns identify and vilify what their own supporters dislike the most about rival candidates, and use this to motivate turnout.[233] "The determination to vote out the opposition, and the broader trend of acute polarization within the American political system, has altered virtually every facet of our political life," Rachel Bitecofer tells us.[234] It is campaigning for the Presidency cast in the most familiar terms of us against a vilified them. Lock her up. Lock him up.

Alan Abramowitz and Steven Webster tell us that since the 1980s, supporters of both the Democratic and Republican parties have grown over time to dislike the

---

233 David Freedlander, "An Unsettling New Theory: There is No Swing Vote." *Politico* Thursday, February 6, 2020.
234 Rachel Bitecofer, "Fear Factor: The Hidden Dynamic That's Transformed Our Politics, and Will Loom Large in the 2020 Race." *The New Republic* Sunday, March 1, 2020, 30–31.

https://doi.org/10.1515/9783111340029-008

opposing party more than they like their own party and its officeholders. "In to-day's environment, rather than seeking to inspire voters around a cohesive and forward-looking vision, politicians need only incite fear and anger toward the opposing party to win and maintain power," Abramowitz and Webster tell us.[235] "Until that fundamental incentive goes away, expect politics to get even uglier." And uglier it has certainly gotten.

In campaigning today, negative partisanship is a world of "they" and "them." "We need to do whatever it takes to keep them from winning." "They'll never give up power if they win this election." "We can't let them win this time." "2024 is the most important election in the history of our country." "If we don't make the right moves in 2024, the nation will fall." Every election becomes a struggle to save the country. Nothing is new here. Then-Vice President Thomas Jefferson's opponents warned of the dire consequences if Jefferson won the presidency in his rematch with President John Adams in 1800. "Citizens, choose your sides," Jefferson's opponents said in 1800. "He is to declare himself permanent," one Federalist paper said in 1800 of the belief that Jefferson would refuse to leave office if he defeated Adams.[236]

"If we don't win this election, we'll lose our country forever." "We must be clear-eyed about the threat we face." "If you don't fight like hell, you're not going to have a country anymore." "Not my President." The language of negative partisanship is the language of despair and of desperation. Every election becomes a moment defined by the threat of the other side and its candidate winning. Think of the word campaign, from the Latin *campus*, translated from its earlies iteration as flat level ground, or a plain or open field, that later became used in military vernacular to define the duration of a military exercise or maneuver.[237] Today, negative partisanship is not warfare's language of winners or losers. It is, rather, one of good or evil. A loss for the other party is a win for us – no matter what it takes and no matter what the cost. Nothing is off limits, everything is fair game, and anything goes. Even the rules of military engagement, such as they are, seem not to apply.

235 Alan Abramowitz and Steven Webster, "Negative Partisanship Explains Everything." *Politico* Friday, September 1, 2017.

236 Susan Dunn, *Jefferson's Second Revolution: The Election Crisis of 1800 and the Triumph of Republicanism.* Houghton Mifflin, 2004, 206.

237 "Campaign comes from the French word for open, level country and evolved from there into the military vocabulary, where it was first used to denote the amount of time an army was kept in the field, and later a particular military operation." William Safire, *Safire's Political Dictionary: An Enlarged, Up-To-Date Edition of The New Language of Politics.* Random House, 1978, 93. Think, too, of a college or a university campus.

The era of negative partisanship is a world of taking sides, of choosing sides, of wining-at-all costs, of winning no matter what. Again, nothing is new here. Politics, as Henry Adams famously said, "has always been the systematic organization of hatreds."[238] "The whole secret of politics – knowing who hates who," Kevin Phillips told Garry Wills in 1968, an angry year in American politics.[239] Democrats and Republicans remind their faithful less of their hopes and more of their fears. Campaigns turn competitors into enemies. "Both sides are casting their ballots with anger, and the question is, which side is angrier?" one MSNBC pundit asked in October 2022 just days before that year's midterm contest. MSNBC coverage of the debt ceiling showdown on Capitol Hill in 2023 took it even further. "November 2024 is shaping up as the battle of, 'who do you hate less?'" an MNSBC host asked in April 2023.

In the era of negative partisanship, elections are more about turnout than persuasion – and turnout is all about anger and fear. "When you're making campaign calculations, you go to the voters you're performing well with more than those you're not winning over," one leading Republican strategist told *Vanity Fair* in April 2023.[240] Winning elections in the era of negative partisanship involves appealing not to a vast shifting center of voters, but hinges on the turnout and mobilization of a smaller, angrier, more motivated electorate. Angry voters are more likely to vote, so the playbook is a scorched-earth, nothing-off-limits approach to campaigning held together by a glue of grievance. "Outrage sells," *The New York Times* tells us in June 2023.[241] Fund-raging and *Roe*-rage is the anger of the age manifest in large-scale, low-dollar, online donations.[242] Social media platforms in the palm of our hands first-thing in the morning when we wake up make it possible for us to be outraged every day almost as soon as we open our eyes as a part of this negative partisanship.

The era of negative partisanship is an era where candidates and elected officials have to be louder, meaner, tougher. Hair-trigger sensitivities and a culture of always-on anger and outrage fuel tense confrontations and microaggressions with

238 Henry Adams, *The Education of Henry Adams: An Autobiography*. Houghton Mifflin Company, 1918, 7.
239 Garry Wills, *Nixon Agonistes: The Crisis of the Self-Made Man*. Houghton Mifflin Company, 1970, 265.
240 Caleb Ecarma, "The Conservative Youth Movement is Still Going Strong, Except at the Polls." *Vanity Fair* Sunday, Thursday, April 6, 2023.
241 Shane Goldmacher, "With Migrant Flights, DeSantis Shows Stoking Outrage is the Point." *The New York Times* Wednesday, June 7, 2023.
242 Paul Kane, "Democrats Capitalize on 'Fundraging' to Dominate G.O.P. Senate Candidates on the Airwaves." *The Washington Post* Sunday, October 24, 2020.

strangers everywhere from streetcorners at rallies and campaign events to online digital platforms. It is the sad, solitary, sullen age of arguing with strangers, as face-to-face gatherings and get-togethers are replaced by hours spent in the workplace and at home on digital platforms in anonymous, escalating arguments with people we'll never know or meet.

Barely-perceptible moments of compromise and moderation still take place in the U.S. Congress, in our state legislatures, our county commissions, city councils, and school boards, but so often these are drown out in speed-of-Twitter news cycles that barely give adversaries a chance to celebrate their crossing-the-aisle before the TV camera-lights go back on, the Tweets are posted, and the digital battle-lines drawn once again. In the era of YouTube, Instagram, Snapchat, and TikTok, trackers with phones and digital video cameras at airports, on sidewalks, and elsewhere catch candidates and elected officials everywhere they go, off-guard, on-the-run, to take advantage of every utterance or aside in a nothing-is-out-of-bounds, nothing-is-off limits age of political paparazzi.

"The bonds that once helped produce political consensus have gradually eroded, replaced by competing campaigns that live in parallel universes, have sharply divergent world views, and express more distrust of opponents than they did decades ago," *The Washington Post* said in October 2013.[243] "Many activists describe the stakes [of elections] in apocalyptic terms," *The Washington Post* reported. Not to be outdone, *The New York Times* in January 2017 lamented ours as "a noisy era of information overload, extreme partisanship, and knee-jerk reactions."[244] A self-absorbed, self-centered, self-satisfied moment in American political life was never more aptly assessed. Tuesday, February 4, 2020's State of the Union address – just weeks after the December 2019 impeachment of President Donald Trump – saw then-Speaker of the House Nancy Pelosi rip her copy of the President's speech in-half on national television, a defining moment of contemporary negative partisanship.

When we think about negative partisanship today in the lead up to Tuesday, November 5, 2024's presidential election, we would do well to remind ourselves that campaigning for the White House and for elected office today is suffused with a superficiality and a staged theatrics that is every bit as important a part of campaigning as the aggrievements of negative partisanship.[245] Today is a time

---

243 Dan Balz, "Shutdown's Roots Lie in Deeply Embedded Divisions in America's Politics." *The Washington Post* Sunday, October 6, 2013.

244 Michiko Kakutani, "Obama's Secret to Surviving the White House Years: Books." *The New York Times* Monday, January 16, 2017.

245 Josh King, *Off Script: An Advance Man's Guide to White House Stagecraft, Campaign Spectacle, and Political Suicide.* St. Martin's Press, 2016.

of artifice and atmospherics, of contrivances and optics in campaigns for the White House that deflect, distract, and disorient an electorate whose hands forever hover over their computer mouses and their cellphone screens in search of the latest snippets of favored candidates "destroying" or "owning" their rivals, snippets that are inevitably accompanied with links pleading for financial contributions.

"It is the age of rage," *Politico* tells us, but it is also the age of staged, theatrical outrage, what I call here a performative partisanship of name-calling, posturing, and stagecraft in riling up one of the most easy-to-rile-up electorates in our country's history, reached instantaneously and unfiltered in the blink-of-an-eye through digital platforms checked incessantly by voters on their cellphones in almost every waking moment of their day.[246] It is a time of "grievance politics," *The Washington Post* tells us, but the grievance is so often contrivance. So much in today's campaigning is empty and fleeting, the drama unnecessary, the brinkmanship meaningless, the posturing pointless.[247] Deliberately provoking fights and pursuing the most unserious targets – Bud Light, Disney, Target – is the new normal in campaigning for the White House, too often replacing carefully-crafted policy positions and thoughtfully-written speeches with showmanship and stunts in the minute-to-minute fight for attention, clicks, and contributions.

Today's road to the White House is built around digital platforms that feed and are fed by the electorate's appetite for the latest outrage by the opposing party's candidates and by the "owning" of these rivals by our own party's candidates. With the most loyal supporters just a thumb-swipe away on their phones, candidates miss no opportunity to fuel their followers' appetite for the latest you-won't-believe-what-I-just-said-about-the-other-side moment. We filter out and focus on the worst stories about the other party, our attention and eyes drawn to the headlines that make us the most angry. Because of this, credibility-straining stands and statements are a must by candidates in both our Democratic and Republican Parties today, the "you-won't-believe-this" and "I-can't-make-this-up" e-mail subject lines, links, and texts quickly posted to digital platforms and social media newsfeeds, one after the other, morning, noon, and night. When we scroll Snapchat, TikTok, YouTube, and other platforms, it's the most sensational headlines, taglines, and graphics that draw us in. "WATCH _____ DESTROY _____," whether it is our candidate taking on a rival, or a reporter or a questioner at a campaign event being put in their place by our candidate. It is the

---

246 Jim Vandehei and John F. Harris, "The Age of Rage." *Politico* Friday, July 23, 2010.

247 Robert Costa, "'It's Depressing, Isn't It?' With Little Protest, G.O.P Succumbs to Trump on Spending." *The Washington Post* Thursday, December 2019.

signal-the-base fire that our candidates fuel with their grandstanding and gratuitous words for one another that marks the era of performative partisanship.[248]

Talking points and positioning, posing and posturing – this is the world of campaigning in the 21st century road to the White House. Teams in campaigns build appearances of their candidates less around the words spoken and the policies proposed than the impressions made, carefully-culling speeches for mere seconds-long snippets for digital platforms. Nothing is new here. What is new, in the era of performative partisanship, is the extremes to which candidates and their teams appear willing to go to cut through the noise and the clutter and the short attention span of voters to catch them with you're-not-going-to-believe-this moments of angry harangues, selective outrage, superficial gestures, and soon-to-be-forgotten gimmicks and stunts. Fill taxpayer-funded buses and flights of undocumented migrants and leave them on the sidewalks and street-corners of Martha's Vineyard, Massachusetts, Sacramento, California, Washington, D.C. and elsewhere. Pick a fight online with a Hollywood celebrity or with a high school student taking a stand against gun violence. Argue online with a 15-year old European climate activist or mock high school students wearing masks at a press conference at the height of the COVID-19 pandemic. Compare public health advocates and their support for common-sense vaccination protocols and procedures to the Holocaust. Nothing and no one is too inconsequential or unimportant if it means stirring up controversy and scoring another round of attention from the public and another successful cycle of clicks and contributions from a campaign's supporters.[249] Tak-

---

248 In March 2023's *The New Republic*, Anne Marie Cox names the moment as few have in this time:

YouTube is littered with excitably titled videos of DeSantis "DESTROYING" all kinds of right-wing nemeses. "Watch Ron DeSantis DESTROYS the Media," "DESANTIS DESTROYS NEWSOM," "Ron DeSantis DESTROYS Tampa Bay Rays After Woke Gun Control Virtue Signal," "DeSantis DESTROYS Woke NHL," "DeSantis DESTROYS CRAZY NANCY," as well as "Ron DeSantis DESTROYS Disney World and ENJOYS It." Did he though? I watched that video—and the others—and I am underwhelmed by the toll of the destruction, and certainly DeSantis's enjoyment of it, at least on a performative level. It's all rehearsed and utterly familiar. His stiff combativeness with the media may play well with a general conservative audience, but what's on display is the belligerence of a guy trying to score points and desperately needing his victories to be confirmed.

Anne Marie Cox, "Ron DeSantis: Overrated." *The New Republic* Tuesday, March 14, 2023.

249 In a January 2023 story on MTV's coverage of campaigning for the White House in the early 1990s, Jim Geraghty in *The Washington Post* tells a larger story of the time as few have:

Maintaining people's interest in politics week after week, month after month, requires convincing them that the stakes are always huge, inescapable, and irreversible. This is the most important election of our lifetime! If we get this one wrong, there's no coming back! The circus of politics means there's never a shortage of doom-scrolling material on your phone. There's always some new outrageous comment, some idiot state legislator you've never heard of proposing someing every argument to the extremes is rewarded in the era of performative partisanship.

Signaling your base is the principal purpose of performative partisanship. Even the dog-whistles of another day are now shouted and yelled at full-volume. Tip-toeing and treading-carefully is replaced by full-throated, top-of-your-lungs stands. "The crazier you act, the more money you raise," one MSNBC host said in June 2023. "It's all gesturing to raise money." Halfhearted gestures and deliberately-provoking political rivals – at one time, these may have drawn editorial outrage by hometown and national newspapers, but who reads these anymore? At one time, these may have led contributors and donors to dry-up their financial support for candidates, but it's the senselessness and shamelessness that is the very draw and driver for many of these donations today. When *The New Yorker* in June 2022 asked its readers in the headline, "Can Ron DeSantis Displace Donald Trump as the G.O.P.'s Combatant-in-Chief," that standout phrase, "Combatant-in-Chief," said it all, for the signaling of the base in taking on opponents to the delight of their supporters, something that happens in both Republican and Democratic campaigns today.[250]

What we know for certain is this. Someone right now is reviewing their ad-copy or their fundraising e-mail or text-message that will call Tuesday, November 5, 2024 the "most important election of our lifetime." A candidate's staff right now somewhere is preparing their urgent appeal for November 2024 with the plea, "we've got to take our country back." This much is certain. Democrats and Republicans alike will call 2024's election "the most important election in our history." The "future of our country" will hang in the balance that November 5th just as it has been said time and time before. With the same urgency that has been said a hundred times before, we'll be told November 2024 is the most important election in our history, with a seriousness that can't be taken seriously, since we are told this in every election and since we well know in the study of our history of America's political parties in our presidential elections that their only constant is this constant refrain.

thing ridiculous and blatantly un-Constitutional. Every day, you can find some evidence to convince yourself that the inmates are now running the asylum, and that you, commonsense-blessed citizen, are an endangered minority.

Jim Geraghty, "How Did Politics Get So Awful? I Blame MTV Circa 1992." *The Washington Post* Sunday, January 8, 2023.

250 Dexter Filkins, "Can Ron DeSantis Displace Donald Trump as the G.O.P.'s Combatant-in-Chief?" *The New Yorker* Wednesday, June 27, 2022.

Reference List

Books, Articles and Chapters

Abramowitz, Alan and Steven Webster. "Negative Partisanship Explains Everything." *Politico* Friday, September 1, 2017.

Adams, Henry. *The Education of Henry Adams: An Autobiography.* Houghton Mifflin Company, 1918.

Adams, John Quincy. *Memoirs of John Quincy Adams, Comprising Portions of His Diary from 1795 to 1848, Volume 7,* ed. Charles Francis Adams. J.B. Lippincott and Company, 1875.

Alberta, Tim. *American Carnage: On the Front Lines of the Republican Civil War and the Rise of President Trump.* HarperCollins, 2019.

Allen, Jonathan and Amie Parnes. *Shattered: Inside Hillary Clinton's Doomed Campaign.* Crown, 2017.

Allen, Jonathan and Amie Parnes. *Lucky: How Joe Biden Barely Won the Presidency.* Random House, 2021.

Allen, Michael. "The Federalists and the West, 1783–1803." *The Western Pennsylvania Historical Magazine* 61, no. 4, October 1978.

Allen, Stephen M. *Origin and Early Progress of the Republican Party in the United States, Together with the History of its Formation in Massachusetts.* Getchell Brothers, 1879.

Argersinger, Peter H. "New Perspectives on Election Fraud in the Gilded Age." *Political Science Quarterly* 100, no. 4, Winter 1985.

Barnes, William. *The Origin and Early History of the Republican Party.* J.B. Lyon Company Printers, 1906.

Baumann, Roland M. "'Heads I Win, Tails You Lose': The Public Creditors and the Assumption Issue in Pennsylvania, 1790–1802." *Pennsylvania History* 44, no. 3, July 1977.

Bemis, Samuel Flagg. "Payment of the French Loans to the United States, 1777–1795." *Current History* 23, no. 6, March 1926.

Bemis, Samuel Flagg. *John Quincy Adams and the Union.* Alfred A. Knopf, 1956.

Binkley, Wilfred E. *The Powers of the President: Problems of American Democracy.* Doubleday, Doran and Company, 1937.

Binkley, Wilfred E. *American Political Parties: Their Natural History.* Alfred A. Knopf, 1943.

Bishop, Bill. *The Big Sort: Why the Clustering of Like-Minded America Is Tearing Us Apart.* Houghton Mifflin Company, 2008.

Bitecofer, Rachel. "Fear Factor: The Hidden Dynamic That's Transformed Our Politics, and Will Loom Large in the 2020 Race." *The New Republic* Sunday, March 1, 2020.

Borden, Morton. *Parties and Politics in the Early Republic, 1789–1815.* Thomas Y. Crowell Company, 1967.

Burner, David. *The Politics of Provincialism: The Democratic Party in Transition, 1918–1932.* Alfred A. Knopf, 1970.

Burner, David. *Herbert Hoover: A Public Life.* Alfred A. Knopf, 1979.

Casey, Ralph D. "Republican Propaganda in the 1936 Campaign." *The Public Opinion Quarterly* 1, no. 2, April 1937.

Chambers, William Nisbet. *Political Parties in a New Nation: The American Experience, 1776–1809.* Oxford University Press, 1963.

Chase, James S. *Emergence of the Presidential Nominating Convention, 1789–1832.* The University of Illinois Press, 1973.

Coletta, Paolo E. *William Jennings Bryan: Political Evangelist, 1860–1908.* The University of Nebraska Press, 1964.

Cox, Anne Marie. "Ron DeSantis: Overrated." *The New Republic* Tuesday, March 14, 2023.

Curtis, Francis. *The Republican Party: A History of its 50 Years' Existence and a Record of its Measures and Leaders, 1854–1904, Volume I.* G.P. Putnam's Sons, 1904.

Dent, Harry S. *The Prodigal South Returns to Power.* John Wiley and Sons, 1978.

Dunn, Susan. *Jefferson's Second Revolution: The Election Crisis of 1800 and the Triumph of Republicanism.* Houghton Mifflin, 2004.

Ecarma, Caleb. "The Conservative Youth Movement is Still Going Strong, Except at the Polls." *Vanity Fair* Sunday, Thursday, April 6, 2023.

Evjen, Henry O. "The Willkie Campaign: An Unfortunate Chapter in Republican Leadership." *The Journal of Politics* 14, no. 2, May 1952.

Filkins, Dexter. "Can Ron DeSantis Displace Donald Trump as the G.O.P.'s Combatant-in-Chief?" *The New Yorker* Wednesday, June 27, 2022.

Flick, Alexander Clarence. *Samuel Jones Tilden: A Study in Political Sagacity.* Kennikat Press, 1939.

Foster, William Omer. *James Jackson: Duelist and Militant Statesman, 1757–1806.* The University of Georgia Press, 1960.

Frank, Jeffrey. *Ike and Dick: Portrait of a Strange Political Marriage.* Simon and Schuster 2013.

Fredman, L.E. Fredman. *The Australian Ballot: The Story of an American Reform.* Michigan State University Press, 1968.

Freedlander, David. "An Unsettling New Theory: There is No Swing Vote." *Politico* Thursday, February 6, 2020.

Gienapp, William E. "Who Voted for Lincoln?" In John L. Thomas (ed.) *Abraham Lincoln and the American Political Tradition.* The University of Massachusetts Press, 1986.

Harlow, Ralph Volney. *The History of Legislative Methods in the Period before 1825.* Yale University Press, 1917.

Hofstadter, Richard. *The American Political Tradition and the Men Who Made It.* Alfred A. Knopf, 1948.

Hollandsworth, James G. *Pretense of Glory: The Life of General Nathaniel P. Banks.* Louisiana State University Press, 1998.

Hollcroft, Temple R. "A Congressman's Letters on the Speaker Election in the Thirty-Fourth Congress." *The Mississippi Valley Historical Review* 43, no. 3, December 1956.

Holt, Michael F. *The Rise and Fall of the American Whig Party: Jacksonian Politics and the Onset of the Civil War.* Oxford University Press, 1999.

Howe, George Frederick. *Chester A. Arthur: A Quarter-Century of Machine Politics.* Dodd, Mead and Company, 1934.

The Documentary History of the First Federal Elections, 1788–1790, Volume I, eds. Merrill Jensen and Robert A. Becker. The University of Wisconsin Press, 1976.

King, Josh. *Off Script: An Advance Man's Guide to White House Stagecraft, Campaign Spectacle, and Political Suicide.* St. Martin's Press, 2016.

Libby, Orin Grant. "A Sketch of the Early Political Parties in the United States." *The Quarterly Journal of the University of North Dakota* 2, no. 3, April 1912.

Libby, Orin Grant. "Political Factions in Washington's Administrations." *The Quarterly Journal of the University of North Dakota* 3, no. 4, July 1913.

Lloyd, Thomas. *The Congressional Register, or History of the Proceedings and Debates of the First House of Representatives of the United States of America, Volume I.* Harrison and Purdy, 1789.

Lloyd, Thomas. *The Congressional Register, or History of the Proceedings and Debates of the First House of Representatives of the United States of America, Volume II.* Hodge, Allen, and Campbell, 1790.

Lomask, Milton. *Aaron Burr: The Years from Princeton to Vice President, 1756–1805.* Farrar Straus Giroux, 1979.

The Diary of William Maclay and Other Notes on Senate Debates, Volume IX, eds. Kenneth R. Bowling and Helen E. Veit. The Johns Hopkins University Press, 1988, 239.

Maney, Patrick J. *The Roosevelt Presence: A Biography of Franklin Delano Roosevelt.* Simon and Schuster, 1992.

Manners, William. *TR and Will: A Friendship that Split the Republican Party.* Harcourt, Brace and World, 1969.

Martis, Kenneth C. *The Historical Atlas of the Political Parties in the United States Congress, 1789–1989.* Macmillan Publishing Company, 1989.

Martz, Larry. "Carter's Coup, Ford's Struggle." *Newsweek* 87, no. 26, Monday, June 21, 1976.

Miller, John C. *The Federalist Era, 1789–1801.* Harper and Brothers Publishers, 1960.

Milton, George Fort. *The Eve of Conflict: Stephen A. Douglas and the Needless War.* Houghton Mifflin Company, 1934.

Montville, Leigh. *The Big Bam: The Life and Times of Babe Ruth.* Doubleday, 2006.

Mowry, George E. "Theodore Roosevelt and the Election of 1910." *The Mississippi Valley Historical Review* 25, no. 4, March 1939.

Nichols, Roy F. *The Invention of the American Political Parties.* The Macmillan Company, 1967.

Official Proceedings of the National Democratic Convention, Held in Cincinnati, June 2–6, 1856. Enquirer Company Steam Printing Establishment, 1856.

O'Neill, Tip. *Man of the House: The Life and Political Memoirs of Speaker Tip O'Neill.* The Bodley Head, 1987.

Parsons, Lynn Hudson. *The Birth of Modern Politics: Andrew Jackson, John Quincy Adams, and the Election of 1828.* Oxford University Press, 2009.

Parsons, Stanley B., William W. Beach and Dan Hermann, *United States Congressional Districts, 1788–1841.* Greenwood Press, 1978.

Paullin, Charles O. "The First Elections under the Constitution." *The Iowa Journal of History and Politics* 2, no. 1, January 1904.

Peirce, Neal R. *The People's President: The Electoral College in American History and the Direct Vote Alternative.* Simon and Schuster, 1968.

Peterson, Merrill D. *Thomas Jefferson and the New Nation: A Biography.* Oxford University Press, 1970.

Reeves, Thomas C. *Gentleman Boss: The Life of Chester Alan Arthur.* Alfred A. Knopf, 1975.

Remini, Robert V. *Martin Van Buren and the Making of the Democratic Party.* Columbia University Press, 1959.

Remini, Robert V. *The Election of Andrew Jackson.* J.B. Lippincott Company, 1963.

Remini, Robert V. *The Revolutionary Age of Andrew Jackson.* Harper and Row Publishers, 1976.

Remini, Robert V. *The Jackson Era.* Harlan Davidson, Inc. 1989.

Remini, Robert V. *Andrew Jackson.* Twayne Publishers, 1996.

Rusk, Jerrold G. "The Effect of the Australian Ballot Reform on Split Ticket Voting, 1876–1908." *The American Political Science Review* 64, no. 4, December 1970.

Safire, William. *Safire's Political Dictionary: An Enlarged, Up-To-Date Edition of The New Language of Politics.* Random House, 1978.

Schattschneider, E.E. *The Semisovereign People: A Realist's View of Democracy in America.* Holt, Reinhart, and Winston, 1960.

Severn, Bill. *Samuel J. Tilden and the Stolen Election.* Ives Washburn, Inc., 1968.

Sharp, James Roger. *American Politics in the Early Republic: The New Nation in Crisis.* Yale University Press, 1993.

Silbey, Joel H. "After 'The First Northern Victory': The Republican Party Comes to Congress, 1855–1856." *The Journal of Interdisciplinary History* 20, no. 1, Summer 1989.

Smith, Alfred E. *The Citizen and His Government.* Harper and Brothers, 1935.

Stanwood, Edward. *James Gillespie Blaine.* Houghton Mifflin and Company, 1905.

Farewell Address, Monday, September 19, 1796, in *The Papers of George Washington, Volume XX, 1 April – 21 September 1796,* eds. Jennifer E. Steenshorne, David R. Hoth, William F. Ferraro, Thomas E. Dulan, and Benjamin L. Huggins. The University Press of Virginia, 2019, 703–718.

Summers, Mark Wahlgren. *The Era of Good Stealings.* Oxford University Press, 1993.

Summers, Mark Wahlgren. "Party Games: The Art of Stealing Elections in the Late-Nineteenth Century Untied States." *The Journal of American History* 88, no. 2, September 2001.

Summers, Mark Wahlgren. "'To Make the Wheels Revolve We Must Have Grease': Barrel Politics in the Gilded Age." *The Journal of Policy History* 14, no. 1, January 2002.

Report Relative to a Provision for the Support of Public Credit, Saturday, January 9, 1790, in *The Papers of Alexander Hamilton, Volume VI, December 1789-August 1790,* eds. Harold C. Syrett and Jacob C. Cooke. Columbia University Press, 1962, 102–103.

Van Buren, Martin. *Inquiry into the Origin and Course of Political Parties in the United States.* Hurd and Houghton, 1867.

Vandehei, Jim and John F. Harris. "The Age of Rage." *Politico* Friday, July 23, 2010.

White, Richard D. *Will Rogers: A Political Life.* Texas Tech University Press, 2011.

Wills, Garry. *Nixon Agonistes: The Crisis of the Self-Made Man.* Houghton Mifflin Company, 1970.

Wilson, Woodrow. *A History of the American People, Illustrated with Portraits, Maps, Plans, Facsimiles, Rare Prints, Contemporary Views, Etc. in Five Volumes, Volume V.* Harper and Brothers Publishers, 1902.

Correspondence

Fisher Ames to Samuel Henshaw, Wednesday, April 22, 1789, in *Documentary History of the First Federal Congress, 1789–1791. Correspondence, First Session: March-May 1789, Volume XV,* eds. Charlene Bangs Bickford, Kenneth R. Bowling, Helen E. Veit, and William Charles DiGiacomantonio. The Johns Hopkins University Press, 2004, 314.

Fisher Ames to James Lowell, Wednesday, April 8, 1789, in *Documentary History of the First Federal Congress, 1789–1791. Correspondence, First Session: March-May 1789, Volume XV,* eds. Charlene Bangs Bickford, Kenneth R. Bowling, Helen E. Veit, and William Charles DiGiacomantonio. The Johns Hopkins University Press, 2004, 221.

Fisher Ames to George R. Minot, Wednesday, July 8, 1789, in *Documentary History of the First Federal Congress, 1789–1791. Correspondence, First Session: June-August 1789, Volume XVI,* eds. Charlene Bangs Bickford, Kenneth R. Bowling, Helen E. Veit, and William Charles DiGiacomantonio. The Johns Hopkins University Press, 2004, 978.

Fisher Ames to Thomas Dwight, Thursday, May 19, 1796, in *Works of Fisher Ames with a Selection from his Speeches and Correspondence, Volume I,* ed. Seth Ames. Little, Brown and Company, 1854, 193–194.

John Beckley to James Madison, Wednesday, October 17, 1792, in *The Papers of James Madison, Volume XIV, 6 April 1791–16 March 1793*, eds. Robert A. Rutland, Thomas A. Mason, Robert J. Brugger, Jeanne K. Sisson, and Fredrika J. Teute. The University Press of Virginia, 1983, 383.

Aedanus Burke to Alexander Hamilton, Wednesday, April 7, 1790, in *The Papers of Alexander Hamilton, Volume VI, December 1789-August 1790*, eds. Harold C. Syrett and Jacob C. Cooke. Columbia University Press, 1962, 358.

James Jackson to James Madison, Friday, May 15, 1801, in *The Papers of James Madison, Secretary of State Series, Volume I, 4 March-31 July 1801*, eds. Robert J. Brugger, Robert Rhodes Crout, Dru Dowdy, Robert A. Rutland, and Jeanne K. Sisson. The University Press of Virginia, 1986, 176.

Abraham Lincoln to Joshua F. Speed, Friday, August 24, 1855, in *The Collected Works of Abraham Lincoln, Volume II*, ed. Roy P. Basler. Rutgers University Press, 1953, 322–323.

Tristram Lowther to James Iredell, Saturday, May 9, 1789, in *Documentary History of the First Federal Congress, 1789–1791. Correspondence, First Session: March-May 1789, Volume XV*, eds. Charlene Bangs Bickford, Kenneth R. Bowling, Helen E. Veit, William Charles DiGiacomantonio. The Johns Hopkins University Press, 2004, 493.

James Madison to Thomas Jefferson, Sunday, March 29, 1789, in *The Papers of James Madison, Volume XII, 2 March 1789–20 January 1790*, eds. Charles F. Hobson, William M. E. Rachal, Robert A. Rutland, and James K. Sisson. The University Press of Virginia, 1979, 38.

James Madison to Thomas Jefferson, Wednesday, May 27, 1789, in *The Papers of James Madison, Volume XII, 2 March 1789–20 January 1790*, eds. Charles F. Hobson, William M. E. Rachal, Robert A. Rutland, and James K. Sisson. The University Press of Virginia, 1979, 186.

James Madison to Henry Lee, Tuesday, April 13, 1790, in *The Papers of James Madison, Volume XIII, 20 January 1790–31 March 1791*, eds. Charles F. Hobson, William M. E. Rachal, Robert A. Rutland, and James K. Sisson. The University Press of Virginia, 1981, 148.

Frederick A. Muhlenberg to Richard Peters, Thursday, June 18, 1789, in *Documentary History of the First Federal Congress, 1789–1791. Correspondence, First Session: June-August 1789, Volume XVI*, eds. Charlene Bangs Bickford, Kenneth R. Bowling, Helen E. Veit, and William Charles DiGiacomantonio. The Johns Hopkins University Press, 2004, 807.

William Smith to Gabriel Manigault, Sunday, June 7, 1789, in *Documentary History of the First Federal Congress, 1789–1791. Correspondence, First Session: June-August 1789, Volume XVI*, eds. Charlene Bangs Bickford, Kenneth R. Bowling, Helen E. Veit, and William Charles DiGiacomantonio. The Johns Hopkins University Press, 2004, 718.

Newspaper Articles

"Mattingly Outruns Talmadge by 22,008." *The Atlanta Constitution* Thursday, November 6, 1980, 1.

"The Presidential Election." *The Charleston Mercury* Wednesday, November 7, 1860, 2.

"The News of Lincoln's Election." *The Charleston Mercury* Thursday, November 8, 1860, 1.

"The Twentieth Day of December, in the Year of Our Lord, 1860." *The Charleston Mercury* Friday, December 21, 1860, 1.

"Cleveland! Democrats Have Scored an Overwhelming Victory, New York State Swings at Tammany's Bidding, Vote in the Upper Counties too Small to Overcome that Below, Indiana Returns Mixed but the Democrats are in the Lead, Later Returns are not Likely to Change the Situation, Slow Returns Caused by the Working of the New Ballot Laws, California Democratic by 7,000." *The Chicago Daily Tribune* Wednesday, November 9, 1892, 1.

"Bryan at the Home of McKinley, He is Given a Respectful Hearing and Compliments His Opponent." *The Chicago Daily Tribune* Tuesday, August 11, 1896, 3.

"Bryan the Idol Smashed by Party, Former Leader on Eighth Anniversary of His Triumph Repudiated by Vote of 647 to 299, Magic Power is Gone, Test Forced by Nebraskan Served to Show how Strong the Parker Sentiment has Grown." *The Chicago Daily Tribune* Friday, July 8, 1904, 1.

"Parker Chosen on First Ballot, Democrats Nominated New York Judge on Platform Agreed to Without any Opposition, Bryan to Support Him, Result is not Reached until Early Hour this Morning and After Much Oratory." *The Chicago Daily Tribune* Saturday, July 9, 1904, 1.

"New Party Opens Convention Today as Colonel Comes, Roosevelt Will Confer with National Progressive Leaders before the Meeting, All Allowed to Talk, Platform Outlined which is Expected to Create New Era in Politics, Beveridge to Give Keynote." *The Chicago Daily Tribune* Monday, August 5, 1912, 1

"Get the Hook for Dems, Al Jolson Sings to Harding, Theater Stars Chase Care at Marion Jubilee." *The Chicago Daily Tribune* Wednesday, August 25, 1920, 9.

"Harding Drives a Few Homers for 'Cub' Guests, Against One Man Team in World League." *The Chicago Daily Tribune* Friday, September 3, 1920, 2.

"Cox Starts 10,000 Mile Speaking Tour of West, In Michigan Today, in Chicago Sunday." *The Chicago Daily Tribune* Friday, September 3, 1920, 2.

"Chicago Listens to Returns Via Radio, Telephone, Voice from Ether Spells End of Former Crowds." *The Chicago Daily Tribune* Wednesday, November 7, 1928, 9.

"Hoover Speeds West to Open Campaign, Gives Fighting Speech Tonight at Des Moines, Hopes He Can Hold G.O.P. Farm Vote." *The Chicago Daily Tribune* Tuesday, October 4, 1932, 1.

"Amendment to End Lame Duck Rule Adopted, 36 States Approve new Law." *The Chicago Daily Tribune* Tuesday, January 24, 1933, 1.

"Landon Keeps Vigil Alone in Victory Hour." *The Chicago Daily Tribune* Friday, June 12, 1936, 1.

"Texan Backing Court Plan Wins Congress Seat." *The Chicago Daily Tribune* Sunday, April 11, 1937, 8.

"F.D.R. to Run, He Reveals it with a Flourish, Seeks a Fourth Term 'Reluctantly.'" *The Chicago Daily Tribune* Wednesday, July 12, 1944, 1.

"President Says Yes from Train on West Coast." *The Chicago Daily Tribune* Friday, July 21, 1944, 1.

"G.O.P. Elephant Taken for Ride by New Dealers, 'Me-Too' Boys are High in the Howdah." *The Chicago Daily Tribune* Wednesday, July 23, 1948, 5.

"Republican Nominations, for President of the United States, Abraham Lincoln of Illinois, for Vice President, Hannibal Hamlin of Maine, for the Great Presidential Campaign." *The Chicago Press and Tribune* Saturday, May 19, 1860, 1.

"Stage Set for Kennedy, Nixon on CBS, Rivals to be Cool, Undistracted." *The Chicago Tribune* Sunday, September 25, 1960, 1.

"Lyndon Pokes Fun at First Primary Vote." *The Chicago Tribune* Wednesday, March 13, 1968, 6.

"Iowa Dems Give Carter Lead in First U.S. Voter Test." *The Chicago Tribune* Tuesday, January 20, 1976, 5.

"Carter, Reagan Clash on Peace and Economy, Anderson, from 300 Miles Away, Disagrees with Both." *The Chicago Tribune* Wednesday, October 29, 1980, 1.

"Ron Gives 'Em Some of Harry's Hell." *The Chicago Tribune* Saturday, October 13, 1984, 3.

"Bush Is Elected President, Democrats Maintain Firm Control of U.S. House and Senate, Dukakis Tells his Supporters, 'We'll Work with Him.'" *The Chicago Tribune* Wednesday, November 9, 1988, 1.

"Final Passage of the Nebraska Bill in the Senate." *The New York Daily Times* Monday, March 6, 1854, 5.

"A Fugitive Slave in Milwaukee, Excitement of the Citizens, the Jail Broken, the Fugitive Rescued, and the Military Ordered Out." *The New York Daily Times* Friday, March 17, 1854, 3.

"The Election of Mr. Banks to the Speakership, Exciting Scenes in the House." *The New York Daily Times* Wednesday, February 6, 1856, 2.

"Democratic National Convention, Fifth and Last Day, the Nominations Made, James Buchanan for President, John C. Breckinridge for Vice President, Exciting Scenes, Speech of Mr. Breckinridge, How the Nominations are Received." *The New York Daily Times* Saturday, June 7, 1856, 1.

"Secession of the Southern Delegations, Davis and Everett Proposed by the Bolters." *The New York Times* Tuesday, May 1, 1860, 1.

"Debate in the House on the Impeachment Resolution, the Resolution Adopted by a Vote of 126 to 47, the President to be Arraigned for Trial Immediately, Gen. Thomas Makes Another Unsuccessful Attempt to Oust Secretary Stanton, Message of the President Defending His Action in Removing Mr. Stanton." *The New York Times* Tuesday, February 25, 1868, 1.

"Governor Hayes' Letter of Acceptance, an Able and Manly State Paper, Intelligent Views on Civil Service Reform, Sound Declarations on the Currency and the School Question, the True Interests of the South Set Forth, no Question Shirked, Evaded, or Ambiguously Treated." *The New York Times* Monday, July 10, 1876, 1.

"The Electoral Tribunal, Florida's Four Votes for Hayes and Wheeler, Decision of the Case by a Vote of Eight to Seven after Ten Hours in Secret Session, No Separate Vote on the Eligibility of Mr. Humphreys, the Reasons Given for the Decision, Character and Incidents of the Debate, the Florida Case Believed to Carry Louisiana, a Joint Meeting of Congress Today to Continue the Count." *The New York Times* Saturday, February 10, 1877, 1.

"Louisiana for Governor Hayes, Action of the Electoral Tribunal, Resolute Refusal to go Behind the Lawful Act of the State, Evidence Beyond the State Certification Excluded, a Proposition to Permit Further Argument Declined by Counsel on Both Sides, the Eight Votes of Louisiana Counted for Hayes and Wheeler by Eight to Seven, a New Democratic Project for Delay." *The New York Times* Saturday, February 17, 1877, 1.

"The Electoral Tribunal, South Carolina for Hayes, Democratic Lawyers and Commissioners Talking to Consume Time, no Arguments on the Republican Side Except by the Objector, Mr. Lawrence, the Democratic Commissioners Evidently Cognizant of the Action of the House, the Disposition to Talk Less Manifest after the Adjournment of the House." *The New York Times* Wednesday, February 28, 1877, 1.

"The New Administration, President Hayes Takes His Seat, a Grand Popular Demonstration, an Event Promising Peace and Prosperity to the County, Washington Aglow with Enthusiasm over the Result of a Bitter Contest, Farewell to the Old and Welcome to the New Administration, the White House Changes Tenants." *The New York Times* Tuesday, March 6, 1877, 1.

"The Convention's Choice, Blaine and Logan to Bear the Republican Standard, Four Ballots for President Taken amid Great Confusion and Excitement, Blaine at Last Gets a Majority of 133, No Opposition Manifested to Logan for Vice President." *The New York Times* Saturday, June 7, 1884, 1.

"Gov. Cleveland Elected, a Very Decided Majority in the Electoral College, New York Gives Cleveland a Plurality of 10,000, Both Connecticut and New Jersey Democratic, Wisconsin Votes for Cleveland by 5,000, Indiana Democratic by 5,000 Majority, the Returns from the West Coming in Very Slowly, Close Votes in Many States, Returns from the South Show no Break in the Democratic Column." *The New York Times* Wednesday, November 5, 1884, 1.

"The National Election, No Determination of the Presidential Fight, New York Very Close, Indiana and New Jersey for Cleveland, the Congress Remains Democratic." *The New York Times* Wednesday, November 7, 1888, 1.

"The Republican National Ticket Victorious, Congress Democratic by a Small Majority, Re-election of Gov. Hill, the State Legislature Republican." *The New York Times* Thursday, November 8, 1888, 1.

"Chart Showing the Official Vote for President, by States and Counties, in 1888." *The New York Times* Saturday, February 23, 1889, 10.

"Cleveland Was the Lion, The Central Figure at a Notable Banquet, He Addresses the Merchants' Association and is Received with Enthusiasm." *The New York Times* Friday, December 13, 1889, 1, 2.

"Complete Popular Vote for Presidential Electors, Tuesday, November 8, 1892." *The New York Times* Tuesday, January 10, 1893, 3.

"Nebraskans To Boom Bryan." *The New York Times* Monday, July 6, 1896, 3.

"Bryan Talks at Canton, Cheers about Equally Divided between Rival Candidates." *The New York Times* Tuesday, August 11, 1896, 3.

"Roosevelt Sweeps North and West and is Elected President, Says He will not Run Again, Will have 325 Electoral Votes, Republican Gains in Congress, Folk, LaFollette, and Douglas win Governorship Fights." *The New York Times* Wednesday, November 9, 1904, 1.

"Roosevelt Triumphant in Ohio, Claims 15 Districts out of the 21, Harmon Wins, two to one, from Wilson, Colonel's Vote 59,054 to Taft's 41,435 with One-Fourth of Returns in, Taft Carries Cincinnati, but Cleveland, which Senator Burton Hoped to Win for Him, Goes to Roosevelt, Taft Men Claim Half, Declare Roosevelt Estimate Exaggerated but Give out No Figures, Fight Won, says Roosevelt, Gets the News at Oyster Bay and Beams with Delight at His Victory." *The New York Times* Wednesday, May 22, 1912, 1.

"Roosevelt, Beaten, to Bolt Today, Gives the Word in Early Morning, Taft's Nomination Seems Assured, Many of Colonel's Delegates will not Follow Him from Convention, Compromise Talk, Too, Taft Strength Grows, Yesterday's Vote, 564 to 510, Believed to Represent the Actual Line-Up, Woman Leads Cheering, Starts a Demonstration for the Colonel that Lasts Almost an Hour, Hadley Shares in it, Root Quells Disorder, Proves a Firm Chairman, but There is a Great Deal of Confusion During the Speeches." *The New York Times* Thursday, June 20, 1912, 1.

"Roosevelt Delegates Go from the Regular to Rump Convention, Gov. Johnson Presides, Scores the National Committee as Thieves and Promises them a Lesson, New Party on Ruins of Old, Pendergast Makes the Nominating Speech He Had Prepared for Regular Convention, Commandment as Platform, It is 'Thou Shalt Not Steal,' Applied to All the Affairs of Life, Wife and Daughters There, News that Bolting Convention was to be Held Drew a Great Crowd and the Police Reserves." *The New York Times* Sunday, June 23, 1912, 7.

"Maniac in Milwaukee Shoots Col. Roosevelt, He Ignores Wound, Speaks an Hour, Goes to Hospital, Would-Be Assassin is John Schrank, Once Saloonkeeper Here, a Maniac on Third Term, Obsessed with Belief That He was Commissioned to Remove Peril to Nation, Had Dream of McKinley, Martyred President, He Says, Told Him that Roosevelt Had Him Slain, Started on Colonel's Trail, Went South after Buying Revolver and Followed Ex-President Closely, Was Baffled in Chicago, Then He Went Early to Milwaukee and Planned Carefully to Make Sure of His Victim." *The New York Times* Tuesday, October 15, 1912, 1.

"Cox to Start Next Week, Tour of West to be Most Extensive of any Presidential Nominee." *The New York Times* Tuesday, August 24, 1920, 3.

"Harding Demands Team Government, Tells Chicago Cubs 'One-Man Team' Muffed and Struck Out in Paris, They Play Game in Marion, Nominee Refuses Plea of Delegation of Teachers, Confers with Senator Knox." *The New York Times* Friday, September 3, 1920, 3.

"Convention Cheers Keynote Attack on Congress, and Praise of Coolidge, Who Dominates the Session, Leaders Hold Night Conference on Second Place, Back Coolidge, says Burton, He Arraigns Legislators in Panegyric of the President, Galleries Voice Approval, League's Court is Upheld, and Coolidge Declared Right in all Clashes with Congress, Third of Seats Empty." *The New York Times* Wednesday, June 11, 1924, 1.

"McAdoo Ahead on Fifteenth Ballot with 479, Smith 305, Governor gains 64 during Day to his Rival's 47, J.W. Davis Third with 61, Adjourn to 10:30 A.M. Today, Battle Lines hold Firm, McAdoo and Smith Fail to Reach Victory in Day of Balloting, Each makes Small Gains, John W. Davis Advances Steadily, His Strength may be Tested Today, 17 Still in the Contest, Silzer of New Jersey, Sweet of Colorado, Kendrick of Wyoming, and Ferris of Michigan Quit." *The New York Times* Tuesday, July 1, 1924, 1.

"How Delegates Took Bryan's Speech, Turmoil and Disorder Prevails, As He Attempts to Push McAdoo, New York Group is Quiet, But Interrupters Were Plenty in Other State Delegations." *The New York Times* Thursday, July 3, 1924, 3.

"McAdoo Men Suggest Meeting Elsewhere, Talk of Asking for Adjournment to Another City if Deadlock Keeps Up." *The New York Times* Friday, July 4, 1924, 2.

"Thrills Come Early in Morning after Session Opens Tamely, Galleries Cheer Steadfast Stand of Smith Supporters and Boo Unyielding McAdoo States, 'Dark Horses' Make Gains after Ralston Goes." *The New York Times* Wednesday, July 9, 1924, 1.

"Davis Is Put over in Wild Stampede, Weary Delegates Jump for Band Wagon and Then All Join Big Demonstration, It Is West Virginia's Day, Convention Pays Tribute to the Men and the State that Gave It the New Leader." *The New York Times* Thursday, July 10, 1924, 1.

"Hoover Formally Notified, Voices Issues, Opposes Dry Law Repeal or Nullification, Favors Hundreds of Millions for Farm Aid, 70,000 Flock to Stadium, Nominee Addresses the Nation Through Radio in Ceremony at Stanford, Sees Prohibition Abuses, Fact Finding Inquiry to Correct Them Proposed, Republican Tariff is Lauded, Intolerance is Denounced, League Cooperation Favored, Tribute to Coolidge as a Great President." *The New York Times* Sunday, August 12, 1928, 1.

"Message Written on Way, Roosevelt Completed Text as the Plane Neared Toledo." *The New York Times* Sunday, July 3, 1932, 9.

"Text of Governor Roosevelt's Speech at the Convention Accepting the Nomination." *The New York Times* Sunday, July 3, 1932, 8.

"Hoover Admits Failure of Prohibition, Declaring for State Control of Liquor, Would Barter War Debts in Trade Deal, Throng Sees Notification, President Goes Beyond His Platform by Urging Dry Law Change, Against Saloon's Return, Federal Check Demanded to Protect Dry States, Democratic Stand Attacked, Ban on Debt Cancellation, Panic Repelled, He Says, Resting Claim for Reelection on Economic Measures." *The New York Times* Friday, August 12, 1932, 1.

"Thirty-Nine States Ratify Amendment Ending 'Lame Duck' Terms, Missouri is thirty-sixth to Vote Change in the Constitution, Effective on October 15, Inaugurations on January 20, Georgia, Utah and Ohio Legislatures Act Too, Term of Roosevelt Cut, Closes a Ten-Year Fight, Senator Norris Hails Result as a Blow to the Rule of Political Machines." *The New York Times* Tuesday, January 24, 1933, 1.

"House Votes Dry Law Repeal 289–121, States Begin Move for Ratification, Lehman Asks Quick New York Action, House has Frenzied Day, Drys Fight for Floor as Debate is Cut Short by Rules Suspension, Wets Gibe at Blanton, He is Booed as He Tells of Threats to Put Him 'on the Spot,' Garner's Gavel is Futile, Rush Copies to States, Printers at Work on Resolution, So 40 Legislatures Now in Session Can Act." *The New York Times* Tuesday, February 21, 1933, 1.

"Text of the Inaugural Address, President for Vigorous Action, 'This is Pre-Eminently the Time to Speak the Truth,' He Says, in Demand that 'the Temple of our Civilization be Restored to the Ancient Truths.'" *The New York Times* Sunday, March 5, 1933, 1.

"Social Security Bill is Signed, Gives Pensions to Aged, Jobless, Roosevelt Approves Measure Intended to Benefit 30,000,000 Persons when States Adopt Cooperating Laws, He Calls the Measure 'Cornerstone' of his Economic Program." *The New York Times* Thursday, August 15, 1935, 1.

"Democrats Adopt Platform Continuing New Deal, Favor Constitutional Amendments, if Necessary, Convention Abrogates Century-Old Two-Thirds Rule, South Bows to Change, Appeased by Promise to Reapportion as Two-Thirds Rule Ends, Fight on Floor Avoided, Committee Instructs Party Heads to Work out New Representation Basis, On Democratic Vote Cast, Southerners Will be Relatively Stronger than Delegates of Less 'Regular' States." *The New York Times* Friday, June 26, 1936, 1.

"Salvos of Cheers Greet President, Serried Banks of Humanity on Field Hang on the Words of His Acceptance Speech, Applaud Mandate Call, Garner Ceremony Speeded to Bring Roosevelt Before Party as Standard-Bearer Again." *The New York Times* Sunday, June 28, 1936, 1, 25.

"At the Opening Sessions of the Twenty-Fourth Republican National Convention in Philadelphia Yesterday." *The New York Times* Tuesday, June 22, 1948, 3.

"Goldwater Says He'll Run to Give Nation a 'Choice,' He Joins G.O.P. Presidential Race with Vow to Hew to His Conservatism, Sees a Hard Contest, Arizonan Planning to Enter New Hampshire Primary, He Chides Johnson." *The New York Times* Saturday, January 4, 1964, 1.

"Big Capital Vote Goes to Johnson, Goldwater Fails to Carry a Single Precinct in City." *The New York Times* Wednesday, November 4, 1964, 3.

"Kennedy to Make Three Primary Races, Attacks Johnson, Challenge Issued, Senators Says only New Leaders can Change Divisive Policies." *The New York Times* Sunday, March 17, 1968, 1.

"Some Republicans Fearful Party Is on Its Last Legs." *The New York Times* Monday, May 31, 1976, 1, 16.

"Vote for President by States." *The New York Times* Thursday, November 6, 1980, 28.

"Sun Smiles on the President, Blowing Kisses and Happy." *The New York Times* Wednesday, January 21, 1981, 28.

"White House Soliciting Tax Support." *The New York Times* Saturday, June 6, 1981, 1, 30.

"Pension Changes Signed into Law, Social Security Rescue Hailed by President at Ceremony on White House Lawn." *The New York Times* Thursday, April 21, 1983, 17.

"Geraldine Ferraro is Chosen by Mondale as Running Mate, First Woman on Major Ticket, 'Difficult' Decision, But Likely Nominee Says Representative from Queens is 'Best.'" *The New York Times* Friday, July 13, 1984, 1.

"Reagan's Margin is 16,876,932 Votes, President's Popular Vote Lead Second Biggest in History, Official Tallies Show." *The New York Times* Saturday, December 22, 1984, 10.

"Vote Aids Kennedy Ally's Effort to Head Democratic Committee." *The New York Times* Friday, February 1, 1985, 19.

"Dissidents Defy Top Democrats, Council Formed, More Conservative Line is Goal of Policy Panel." *The New York Times* Friday, March 1, 1985, 1.

"Nominees Wage Intensified War of Attack Ads." *The New York Times* Monday, October 10, 1988, 1.

"Democrats Keep Solid Hold on Congress." *The New York Times* Wednesday, November 9, 1988, 24.

"Arkansas' Clinton Enters the '92 Race for President." *The New York Times* Friday, October 4, 1991, 10.

"Clinton Wins a Majority for Nomination but Perot's Appeal Is Strong in Two Parties, Final Six Primaries, Easy Victories for Bush Diluted by Signs of Outsider's Power." *The New York Times* Wednesday, July 3, 1992, 1, 16.

"Perot Re-Enters the Campaign, Saying Bush and Clinton Fail to Address Government 'Mess,' Faces Lag in Polls, Negotiators for Parties Report Agreement on Series of Debates." *The New York Times* Friday, October 2, 1992, 1.

"An Eccentric but No Joke, Perot's Strong Showing Raises Questions on What Might Have Been, and Might Be." *The New York Times* Thursday, November 5, 1992, B4.

"Election Turnout Highest since '68, 55.23% Figure is Attributed Mostly to Perot's Appeal, Except in the South." *The New York Times* Thursday, December 17, 1992, B16.

"Clinton Elected to a Second Term with Solid Margins Across U.S., G.O.P. Keeps Hold on Congress, Democrats Fail to Reverse Right's Capitol Hill Gains." *The New York Times* Wednesday, November 6, 1996, 1.

"Perot Supporters Concentrate on Their Goals for the Future." *The New York Times* Wednesday, November 6, 1996, 34.

"Obama's Secret to Surviving the White House Years: Books." *The New York Times* Monday, January 16, 2017.

"Americans at the Gates: The Trump Era's Inevitable Denouement." *The New York Times* Thursday, January 2, 2021, 1.

"With Migrant Flights, DeSantis Shows Stoking Outrage is the Point." *The New York Times* Wednesday, June 7, 2023.

"Questions Fly at Roosevelt at First Press Conference, Written Procedure Eliminated by President and Correspondents Applaud at Close of Session Lasting 40 Minutes, Executive Frank and Cordial." *The Washington Post* Thursday, March 9, 1933, 3.

"Reagan Says G.O.P. Needs New Name and New Support." *The Washington Post* Saturday, November 20, 1976, 13.

"President, on a Note of Bipartisanship, Signs Social Security Bill." *The Washington Post* Thursday, April 21, 1983, 10.

"Democrats Building Capitol Hill Headquarters." *The Washington Post* Saturday, April 23, 1983, F3.

"Gov. Clinton Wears Out Welcome with Nominating Speech." *The Washington Post* Thursday, July 21, 1988, 27.

"G.O.P. Offers a 'Contract' to Revive Reagan Years." *The Washington Post* Wednesday, September 28, 1994, 1.

"Shutdown's Roots Lie in Deeply Embedded Divisions in America's Politics." *The Washington Post* Sunday, October 6, 2013.

"Shutdown's Roots Lie in Deeply Embedded Divisions in America's Politics." *The Washington Post* Sunday, October 6, 2013.

"'It's Depressing, Isn't It?' With Little Protest, G.O.P Succumbs to Trump on Spending." *The Washington Post* Thursday, December 2019.

"Democrats Capitalize on 'Fundraging' to Dominate G.O.P. Senate Candidates on the Airwaves." *The Washington Post* Sunday, October 24, 2020.

"Trump Impeached Again, 232 to 197, Senate Trial Is Likely to Occur After Departure." *The Washington Post* Thursday, January 14, 2021, 1.

"How Did Politics Get So Awful? I Blame MTV Circa 1992." *The Washington Post* Sunday, January 8, 2023.

Newspaper Issues

Gazette of the United States Saturday, April 18, 1789, 3.

Gazette of the United States Saturday, May 2, 1789, 3.

Gazette of the United States Wednesday, September 30, 1789, 3.

Gazette of the United States Saturday, January 9, 1790, 3.

Gazette of the United States, Wednesday, April 14, 1790, 2.

Gazette of the United States Saturday, April 17, 1790, 3.

Gazette of the United States Wednesday, March 2, 1791.

Gazette of the United States Wednesday, June 8, 1791, 3.

Gazette of the United States Saturday, January 5, 1793, 3.

Gazette of the United States Saturday, February 16, 1793, 2.

Gazette of the United States Wednesday, March 13, 1793, 3.

Massachusetts Centinel, 20 December, in *The Documentary History of the First Federal Elections, 1788–1790, Volume I,* eds. Merrill Jensen and Robert A. Becker. The University of Wisconsin Press, 1976, 570.

Index

Note: References following "n" refer notes.